WRITERS AND THEIR WORK

ISOBEL ARMSTRONG
General Editor

ARTHUR HUGH CLOUGH

Arthur Hugh Clough

from an 1860 portrait in chalk by Samuel Rowse by courtesy of
the National Portrait Gallery, London

ARTHUR HUGH CLOUGH

John Schad

NORTHCOTE
BRITISH
COUNCIL

© Copyright 2006 by John Schad

First published in 2006 by Northcote House Publishers Ltd, Horndon, Tavistock, Devon, PL19 9NQ, United Kingdom.
Tel: +44 (0) 1822 810066 Fax: +44 (0) 1822 810034.

British Library Cataloguing-in-Publication Data
A catalogue record for this book is available from the British Library

ISBN 0-7463-1161-3 hardcover
ISBN 0-7463-1166-4 paperback

Typeset by PDQ Typesetting, Newcastle-under-Lyme
Printed and bound by CPI Group (UK) Ltd, Croydon, CR0 4YY

To Robin and Rosemary

Contents

Acknowledgements

I must, in the first instance, thank Isobel Armstrong for allowing me to write this book. In the first Writers and their Work series it was Isobel who wrote the volume on Clough; hers was a very hard act to follow but, nevertheless, to do so has been a privilege and pleasure. Talking of privilege and pleasure I must also thank my parents-in-law Robin and Rosemary for all their wonderful hospitality; most of this book was written in Wilton. Once it was written, or at least drafted, both Roger Ebbatson and Adam Roberts very nobly read the book, made many excellent suggestions, and spared me from a whole number of embarrassments. Also helpful in this respect was that 'canny vicar' the Rev. John Vickers. Any remaining errors should be attributed to all those who ask me to do wholly unnecessary things, like taking the rubbish out or driving them to a friend's; usual suspects, I'm afraid, namely: Katie, Bethan, Thomas and that 'infant phenomenon', Rebecca.

Biographical Outline

1819   1 January: born in Liverpool, the second son of James Butler Clough, cotton merchant, and Ann Perfect.

1822   Family emigrates to Charleston, South Carolina.

1828   Returns to England to attend school at Chester.

1829   Enters Rugby school with his elder brother, Charles.

1836   July: family returns to England and settles in Liverpool. October: wins scholarship to Balliol College, Oxford.

1837   Enters Balliol.

1841   June: fails to get expected first-class degree. Elected Fellow of Oriel College, Oxford. June: death of Dr Arnold, headmaster of Rugby.

1844   October: father dies.

1847   November: invites Ralph Waldo Emerson to Oxford. December: begins negotiations with the Provost of Oriel, regarding resignation of fellowship.

1848   February: revolution breaks out in France. May–June: with Emerson in revolutionary Paris. October: resigns his fellowship. November: publication of *The Bothie of Toper-na-Fuosich*.

1849   January: publication of *Armbarvalia* (includes poems by Thomas Burbidge). April–July: in Rome during the French siege; writes first draft of *Amours de Voyage*. September: takes up appointment as Principal of University Hall, London.

1850   August–September: visits Venice; writes first draft of *Dipsychus and the Spirit*. December: appointed Professor of English Language and Literature at University College, London.

1851   June(?): meets Blanche Smith, his wife to be.

1852   January: resigns his post at University Hall. June: becomes engaged to Blanche Smith. October: sails for New England.

1853   July: returns from United States and becomes Examiner in the Education Office, London.

1854   June: marries Blanche Smith. October: escorts Florence Nightingale to Calais on her way to the Crimea.

1855   April: first child (a boy) is born but dies a few hours later.

1856   Travels across Europe, inspecting military academies.

1858   February: daughter, Florence, is born. February–May: *Amours de Voyage* is published serially in the *Atlantic Monthly*.

1859   Publication in the United States of *Plutarch's Lives: The Translation Called Dryden's*, corrected from the Greek by A. H. Clough. December: son, Arthur, is born.

1860   June: mother, Ann, dies.

1861   Becomes ill; travels in Europe; writes 'Mari Magno'. August: daughter, Blanche Athena, is born. 13 November: Clough dies in Florence.

1862   Publication in London and Boston of *Poems of Arthur Hugh Clough*.

1865   First publication of *Dipsychus and the Spirit*.

1869   Publication of *Poems and Prose Remains*.

Note on the Text

All quotations for Clough's poetry are taken from *The Poems of Arthur Hugh Clough*, 2nd edition, ed. F. L. Mulhauser (Oxford: Oxford University Press, 1974). All reference details appear as endnotes in order to keep the text as clean and as uncluttered as possible.

We have a foreboding that Clough will be thought a hundred years hence to have been the truest expression in verse of the moral and intellectual tendencies . . . of the period in which he lived.

(James Russell Lowell, 1899)

Introduction – A Thin Poet

> Literary history will hardly care to remember or to
> register the fact that there was a bad poet named Clough,
> whom his friends found it useless to puff: for the public,
> if dull, has not quite such a skull as belongs to believers in
> Clough.
>
> (Charles Algernon Swinburne, 1891)[1]

Swinburne is right, Clough is a bad poet – so bad that he has not had
a whole book written about him for over thirty years; could
never make a living out of his poems; and rarely bothered, it
was said, to talk about poetry.[2] Moreover (and this makes him a
very bad poet) he seems to have valued ideas more than words.
'The "Iliad" ', he writes, 'is but the scum of the mind of Homer,
and Plato's dialogues the refuse of his thought'; words, for
Clough, are merely the rubbish left over after the main event
that is thinking.[3]

  Swinburne is also right to say Clough is dull – he writes about dull
things like rain, lunch and railway guides; and he did dull jobs,
like working as a private tutor, as an Examiner in the Education
Office, and as Florence Nightingale's secretary. He was also
interested in the dull subject of poetic metre, so much so that
when, at a gathering which included Alfred Tennyson, the topic
of conversation moved to prosody, Tennyson turned to Clough
and asked: 'Well, good man Dull, what have you to say?'[4]

  Well, 'good man Dull' has a lot to say. For a start he has much
to say about being dull, being bad and, above all, about being a
failure. When, to everyone's astonishment, he failed to get a
First at Oxford, he famously walked all the way to Rugby to
announce: 'I have failed.' Clough echoes this sentiment as, later
in life, he fails to get a series of academic posts, fails to set up a

1

school in America, and fails to live beyond the age of 42. (Clough died following an ill-defined nervous breakdown caused, to some extent, by the sheer exhaustion of endlessly folding letters and making up parcels for Florence Nightingale).[5] Clough, though, was a failure waiting to happen; as early as 1838 at the age of just 18 he asks himself: 'Is it true that my time of ripening was October –35, & that all I can now do is [a] sort of late gathering up [of] the fragments?'[6] The answer is probably 'Yes', Clough is (quite wonderfully) a poet of fragments, or bits. In this respect, Clough is a bit of a modernist, a bit like T. S. Eliot in *The Waste Land* (1922) who talks of 'fragments I have shored against my ruins'.[7] Clough is also a bit like a 1930s poet, a bit like W. H. Auden, a poet who is bad enough, or unpoetical enough, to put politics before poetry. Clough was known as 'Citizen Clough', supported the Chartists, helped at a night-shelter for vagrants, spoke up for starving Irish peasants, went to see revolutionary Paris, and just happened to be in Rome when it was besieged by the French for two long and bloody months.

This last, accidental brush with history comes just six months after Clough, by now an infamous doubter, feels compelled to leave Anglican Oxford. No wonder the very first poem Clough writes after Oxford includes, as if by way of confession:

> I have so many things to think of, all of a sudden;
> I who had never once thought a thing,–[8]

Once Clough starts thinking, his thoughts come so fast he can scarcely order, or gather them up: 'I mix', he writes, 'all the things I . . . think of.'[9] Indeed, because Clough thinks about so many things – from angels to assassins, beggars to bayonets, streets to signatures – the ensuing mix, or jumble, of thoughts is at times overwhelming. As a dull literary critic I have, predictably, tried to gather up these thoughts into three chapters: the first concentrating on the thought of God; the second on the thought of history; and the third on the thought of death. Though each chapter, at times, glances right across Clough's oeuvre, they are each primarily concerned with a specific period or moment in Clough's life. The first chapter focuses on Clough's Oxford years, 1837 to 1848; the second on his visits to both Paris and Rome in the wake of the revolutionary events of 1848; and the third on the last eleven, fitful years of Clough's life, years marked by professional restlessness and an abortive attempt to settle in America. In this last chapter, the dominant thought, the thought of death, proves to be haunted by the thought of thought. In the end, for Clough, 'thought/ Wheels round on thought'.[10]

When Cloughean thought wheels or turns upon itself it becomes self-involved, even secretive. The American journalist W. J. Stillman, who met Clough in the last year of his life, once wrote that 'there seemed to be in him an *arcanum* of thought', a *mystery or secret* of thought.[11] To read Clough often feels as if you are entering that secret, and finding, or even thinking, thoughts that have not been thought for well over a hundred years. At times, these thoughts almost feel like thoughts that Clough himself never quite got round to thinking. In an early poem Clough cries, 'let me think *my* thought', for he knows that this is far easier said than done, that his thoughts are not necessarily his own, that instead he is prey to what he variously calls 'half-thoughts', 'counter-thoughts', and 'after-thoughts'.[12] These after-thoughts include the thoughts of those who read Clough long after he has died. In Clough, we sense that no thought is complete or finished; that, instead, all thoughts are somehow shared with those not yet even born. In the poem 'Adam and Eve' Clough has Eve declare,

> Methinks
> The questionings of ages yet to be
> The thinkings and cross-thinkings. . .
> . . .
> Of multitudinous souls on souls to come
> In me imprisoned fight, complain, and cry.[13]

Eve knows she does not think alone, as does Clough: 'Yet may *we* think', he writes.[14] Clough invites us not so much to think *about* him as to think *with* him, or even *through* him. In this sense George Saintsbury, writing in 1896, was in fact right to sneer that Clough was not so much a 'bad poet [as] a thin one'; Clough is thin enough to see through, or think through.[15] This effaced and effacing poet does not get in the way of the world, or worlds, of which he writes.

And Clough writes of many worlds, but perhaps the most important to this study is what Clough himself called 'our European world of thought'.[16] Clough, whose early childhood was spent in America, is a poet who, for all his well-performed Englishness, often needs to leave England in order to think: it is 'in a strange land [that] . . . I sit and think'.[17] And there is no stranger land than the world of continental thought, a world in which thought is pushed to the very limit; this was the world of such daring thinkers as Spinoza, Kant, Hegel, Feuerbach, and Strauss, whose work was (in each case) well known to Clough. This was a world where one 'tremble[s] in thinking', where 'trembling thinkers on the brink/ Shiver, and know not how to think'.[18] This is thinking to the point at which 'the brain is sick with thinking', and thought grows so strange as almost to become something else altogether.[19] As we shall see, in Clough, at certain moments, thought becomes indistinguishable from, variously: God, history, and death. But there are still other twists and turns; for, in Clough, thought can become almost anything, even something as strange and unlikely as, say, forgiveness. Perhaps the oddest, most arresting phrase in the whole of Clough is: 'who thinks, forgives'.[20]

Clough certainly thinks; let us hope that in so doing he forgives all those who call him dull. The dull man has a lot to say, particularly about thinking, not least the almost priestly words:

Yet may we think, and forget, and possess our souls in resistance.[21]

These are words to be heeded by those who still wish to think today, in particular those who still wish to think within universities, or 'the academy' as we fondly call it. Clough, we should never forget, had the courage to give up the academy (and, with it, financial security) just as soon as he realized that the academy would no longer allow him to think freely. This freedom is, for very different reasons, once again under enormous pressure. The thin poet is a timely poet.

1

In the Street: The Thought of God

FAST

> Why should I say I see the things I see not,
> Why be and be not?
> Show love for that I love not, and fear for what I fear not?
> And dance about to music that I hear not?
> Who standeth still i' the street
> Shall be hustled and jostled about.[1]

To doubt when all around appear to believe is to be still when everyone else is moving, the only one not dancing – or at least so it seems to Clough writing in 1845. It is a vision that has been with him since at least 1839, when he writes of a 'doubting soul [that], from day to day,/ Uneasy paralytic lay'.[2] This paralytic doubter, or stock-still agnostic is Clough himself; this is Clough in Oxford at a time when the university was overwhelmed by religious movement, in particular a movement called the Oxford Movement – that dramatic burst of High Church energy which, from 1833 to 1845, sought to recall the Church of England to the ancient rites and traditions of Catholicism.[3] For Clough, the Oxford Movement is, indeed, movement: writing to a friend in 1841, he declares, 'you have no idea how fast things here are going Rome-wards'.[4]

Clough refers, in part, to those at Oxford who were in the process of converting from Anglicanism to Catholicism; Clough himself, though, was undergoing a process of *de*conversion, or *un*conversion. Or perhaps we should say an *inverted* conversion, since in 1848 Clough writes, intriguingly, of 'an inverse Saul'.[5] The Saul that Clough has in mind is King Saul of the Old

5

Testament, but by 1848 Clough is very obviously an inverse of the New Testament Saul, the Saul who famously becomes Paul after a dramatic and sudden conversion.[6] Clough's *unconversion* is, though, far from sudden. When he arrived at Oxford in 1837 he was very much a product of the Low Church evangelicalism of his mother and the Broad Church orthodoxy of Thomas Arnold, Clough's headmaster at Rugby; these influences are everywhere in Clough's undergraduate Oxford diaries, and it is not until the early 1840s, with the new theology or 'Higher Criticism' which was coming from Germany, that Clough began to question the historical validity of the Bible.[7] This was a questioning which finally led him, in 1848, to abandon Oxford. Clough's beliefs were no longer in line with the Thirty-Nine Articles, the doctrinal summary of Anglican belief to which all Oxford Fellows were then required to subscribe.

Clough, the undergraduate believer, echoes the evangelicalism of his mother by talking, in his diary, of 'Immediate Conversion' – an event he later parodies as merely 'quick conversion'.[8] The contrasting slowness of Clough's *unconversion* is astonishingly expressed in the second line of a strange two-line poem called 'Irritability Unnatural'; here Clough talks of the

slow, sure poisons [that] wrought God's death's work, God's doom.[9]

We tend to think that God did not die until 1882 when Friedrich Nietzsche, or rather his fictional 'Madman', declares that 'God is dead'; however, the more conventional German philosopher, G. W. F. Hegel makes exactly the same pronouncement as early as 1827.[10] In Victorian England the death of God was still, though, a daring and scandalous motif, even amongst unbelievers; this alone could explain why 'Irritability Unnatural' does not go beyond its second line and was never published by Clough. In this sense, its inordinately long account of the 'slow, sure poisons [that] wrought God's death's work, God's doom' is almost literally interminable, or unfinished. The slow poisons that wrought God's death are, it seems, so slow that God is not so much dead as dying, or even that he has some kind of continuing life, or afterlife. That is certainly the thought, or under-thought of another difficult line written in the same period: namely, 'God, unidentified, was thought-of still.'[11] A God who is 'thought-of *still'* must haunt the unbeliever who 'standeth still'; and so he does, in that the God of Clough's poems is *still* in both senses of the word. Clough writes, 'though aside I start,/ ...still Thou art'.[12] He also writes, of 'the still-still-calling voice/ Of God' which echoes the differently 'still' voice of Elijah's God – the 'still small voice' that Clough recalls in a later poem.[13]

Clough's God is both still and still, both continuing and yet unmoving. For Clough, the mystery of God is somehow bound up with the mystery of movement. It is a mystery most famously expressed by Zeno's 'arrow paradox'; Zeno, the Greek philosopher, argued that since an arrow must occupy a determinate space at each instant in its flight it must, at that instant, be at rest as it flies, and if it is at rest it cannot be in motion. The question of movement is also on the mind of Clough's contemporaries. In 1849 Søren Kierkegaard, the Danish thinker, writes that 'in the life of the spirit there is no standing still'.[14] In the same year, in a letter to Clough, J. A. Froude quotes John Henry Newman's assertion that, as to whether the earth goes around the sun or vice versa, the true believer 'shall never know which is true till we know what *motion* is'.[15] Clough himself alludes precisely to this question when, at the very beginning of his great poem of movement, *Amours de Voyage*, he employs, as an epigraph, the words 'Solvitur ambulando', meaning 'It is refuted by walking', the common-sense Roman response to Zeno's insistence on the logical impossibility of motion.[16] For Zeno, motion is primarily a philosophical question, but for the imaginative Clough, caught as he is in the 'fast-going' world of the Oxford Movement, the paradox of motion is (almost unwittingly) re-imagined as a religious question, as another way of thinking about the paradox of God. In one particular letter, Clough mentions bidding 'God's Speed' to a departing friend; the phrase is conventional but, for Clough, there is a buried fascination with the question of God's speed: does God, to put it simply, move quickly or slowly?[17] This absurd question begins to make some sense when we note that, in a diary entry for 22 February 1838, the undergraduate Clough writes, 'May God help me to make [tomorrow] ... something of a fast-day'; the next day he records that it had been 'not at all a fast day'.[18] Clough refers to the religious act of fasting, but just a month later he laments how, in spiritual terms, he is 'going fast down the hill,' or 'living much too fast'.[19] Clough, we might say,

7

prays for a 'fast day' in order that he might *not* go fast. God's speed is difficult to measure; or at least so it appears in the curiously fast-fast world of the young Clough's letters and diaries.

Admittedly, this world is largely an accident of language: when Clough the young diarist writes, variously, 'have been living … too fast', 'must keep fast' and indeed 'hold fast', he is using one word but in three quite different senses.[20] Clough the poet, however, is well aware of what he calls 'the plethora of possibilities thrown up by language'.[21] He is also aware of the bizarre anomalies and contradictions that emerge as soon as the question of *what motion is* overlaps with the question of *what Christianity is*. Witness *Amours de Voyage*, where Claude is in Rome and sees the stunning pagan statues of the city's ancient past set alongside the Christian monuments of the city's more recent past; addressing the pagan statues that seem as if to move, Claude asks: 'Ye … that …/ Stand … in the grace of your *motionless movement/* …/ Are ye Christian too?'[22] This is a question about Christianity and Paganism; but it is also a question about Christianity and physics – namely, *can* Christianity accommodate paradoxical, or disorderly notions of movement? And that is precisely the question which was beginning to be posed by contemporary physics, in particular the Second Law of Thermodynamics which was formulated in 1847 and argued that entropy, or disorder, will always tend to increase.[23] For almost the first time, the Newtonian account of the world as God's rule-governed, rational machine was beginning to be put under real pressure. The obvious question was: could God be responsible for a disorderly, or irrational world? Or rather: could the Christian mind cope with such illogic? For Clough, in his review of Francis Newman's book *The Soul* (1849), the answer might seem to be 'No'; praising Newman, or the consistency of his Christian life, Clough declares that Newman's

> mind is not a railway with one line … up and the other … down; he is not content to travel one … towards Zion and [the other] … towards Babylon; he has set his face to a single definite terminus.[24]

Here, Clough seems to see the Christian mind as something that simply does not go in two directions at once; but later in the same review, that is exactly what he appears to be looking for. In a strong attack upon overly confident believers, upon those who 'have found out God', Clough launches into a discourse upon the radical uncertainties of contemporary physics:

> Ah, my friends, gravitation is discovered; and behold, a law within the law, a something that is interior to it ... begins to be talked of!... Ptolemy ...thought he had made it out, ... [and then] behold the perfect Newtonian, which explains all! [But] ... the world has not done congratulating itself on moving ... around an established centre ... when lo, the centre is no centre, there is another somewhere – a centre of centres ... We touch the line which we thought our horizon.... We approach, and behold, leagues away, and receding and receding yet again beyond each new limit of the known, a new visible unknown.[25]

The implication is obvious – Clough's believing contemporaries may feel that they have found out God but such confidence is as foolish as the certainty of the Newtonian. If Clough's account of Francis Newman's unilinear, one-way mind is, in effect, a Newtonian account of the Christian mind, here Clough is bordering upon a post-Newtonian theology. Both the world of matter and the world of the spirit are, it seems, capable of logical contradiction; in the next paragraph Clough's declaration that, in physics, 'the centre is no centre' is echoed by the assertion that, in Christianity, 'the Kingdom of God is within us, but it is also without us'. Clough's God violates Newtonian laws of space – he is both within us and without; he is, as it were, both here *and* there. As Clough writes in 'The New Sinai', 'here is God, and there is God! .../ "He is ... here, and here, and here." '[26] This is, in one sense, Clough's own agnostic cry; but, primarily, Clough is here ventriloquizing, or parodying, the believer's claim *to know* where God is, in particular J. H. Newman's claim to know that God is in Rome – the poem is, in part, about Newman's infamous abandonment of Oxford for Catholicism in 1845. So too is *Amours de Voyage*, where Claude declares that 'No, the Christian faith, as I, at least, understood it/ .../ Is not here, O Rome'.[27]

Amours de Voyage is written after Clough's own departure from Oxford. For Clough, the Christian faith is not in Catholic Rome, but neither is it in Anglican Oxford. In short, God is neither here nor there, which is precisely the cry of 'Easter Day, Naples 1849', where Clough, after announcing that 'Christ is not risen', declares that 'Him neither here nor there ye e'er shall meet with more'.[28] Indeed, Clough himself is neither here nor there. In a letter from Oxford in January 1846 he playfully writes, 'I am here. Self-evident proposition!' – it is not, though, such a self-evident proposition, since by this time Clough is already thinking of resigning his fellowship.[29] For Clough, the question of God is now quite literally a question of movement. It is at this point that he describes himself as one who 'standeth still i' the street', as one completely overcome by the sheer (im)possibility of moving. But then, as Clough reminds us, philosophical riddles about motion are to be 'refuted by walking' (*solvitur ambulando*). In Clough's case that meant walking out of Oxford, which is what he did in May 1848.

OUT

> I recommend [you] to walk away ... from this Seat and Citadel of Orthodoxy.[30]
>
> (Clough to J. P. Gell, 16 February 1839)

In May 1848 Clough did not literally walk out of Oxford, but his dramatic departure echoes the famous occasion when he did do so. This was back in June 1841 when, after failing to get the first-class degree that everyone had expected of him, Clough walked alone all the way from Oxford to Rugby to see Thomas Arnold, his old headmaster; years later Tom Arnold (the headmaster's second son) recalls Clough standing in the court of the school-house 'with face partly flushed and partly pale, and saying simply, "I have failed." '[31] Clough, in his diary, recalls how he also walked all the way back to Oxford; but even when returning to Oxford Clough is somehow walking *away* – as early as November 1839 Clough describes how, after one particular journey out, he '*walked* ... the whole distance [back] to Oxford [just in order] ... to be as long out of Oxford as possible'.[32] Clough is simultaneously walking both *to* Oxford and *away from* Oxford.

But then, to leave Oxford at this time *was* an ambiguous act, an act that could (as for Clough) mean doubt, but that could also (as for Newman) mean faith – faith in Rome. Indeed, precisely what Oxford itself meant was in question; the spring of 1848 saw not only Clough's resignation but also a motion in Parliament successfully proposing a Royal Commission Inquiry into

Oxford.[33] The young Clough talks of 'the grandness of the *idea*' of Oxford, but by 1848 many are more concerned with the *question* of Oxford; in particular, the question of whether it is, as the young Clough assumes, a 'Christian university' or, alternatively, as Tom Arnold claimed, a 'kingdom of Darkness'.[34] Just weeks before finally leaving Oxford, Clough asks where he will end up: 'whither', he writes, '[will] the emancipated spirit ... wing its flight ... Paradise or purgatory?'[35] Is to walk out of Oxford an act of *un*conversion or *re*conversion? The young and devout Clough certainly records what reads like some kind of conversion experience when, in March 1842, he walks east out of Oxford; in his diary he writes, enigmatically, that 'when I got to Headington Hill [I] took in the idea of God's love'.[36] For Headington Hill read Damascus Road? The Clough that walks out of Oxford is a Saul as well as an 'inverse Saul', someone who is finding faith as well as losing it.

The same may be said of the Clough who, just a year later, walks into Naples. In the twin poems 'Easter Day, Naples 1849' and 'Easter Day II' Clough walks 'the great sinful streets of Naples'; as he does so he seems first to renounce the Resurrection and then to affirm it. The refrain of the first poem is: 'This is the one sad Gospel that is true,/ Christ is not risen'; the refrain of the second is: 'In the great Gospel and true Creed,/ He is yet risen indeed; / Christ is yet risen'.[37] There is no obvious reason for this seeming reconversion – nothing seems to have changed: in the first poem he is walking the streets of Naples, in the second poem he is walking the streets of Naples. It is as if he has somehow walked his way to faith, or at least a kind of faith. Some things can, it seems, be resolved by walking; or rather, by walking *with another* – the one clue we have as to the change of mind is that the second poem begins with the words: 'the blear-eyed pimp beside me walked'.[38] Clough no longer walks alone. We learn very little about this shadowy companion, and nothing about how he might change Clough's view of the Resurrection; however, as Bible-reading Victorians would know, to fall into step with a stranger was one way in which the first disciples learnt that Christ was risen. This is the story of the 'Emmaus inn' of which we are reminded in the first poem, the story of the two disciples who are walking to Emmaus after the Crucifixion, convinced that everything is finished; they are then joined by a stranger who walks beside them, a stranger who turns out to be the resurrected Christ.[39] The blear-eyed pimp who 'beside me walked' on Easter Day is, then, a kind of Christ, a cryptic double of Jesus the friend of sinners – the Jesus who was particularly notorious for befriending prostitutes. In the figure of the pimp, Christ has a mere walk-on part in the Easter story, or at least in Clough's re-imagining of that story, for Clough is busy re-imagining the Resurrection in non-transcendental, humanistic terms. In Clough's 'true Creed', Christ is risen even 'though He return not, [even] though/ He lies and moulders low'; Christ is risen in and through the stubborn persistence of human life.[40] 'Christ is yet risen' in the sense that, as Clough also insists, 'Life yet is Life.'

Humanistic revision of Christianity was a feature of the period; again, the main source was the new German theology with its insistence that the Gospel narratives be demythologized, that the miracles should not be taken literally. The Gospels should still be read, it was argued, but their significance would no longer be as history but as myths, myths that reveal profound truths about the goodness of Man as well as God. As Clough writes in a letter to his sister Anne in May 1847:

> I cannot feel sure that a man may not have all that is important in Christianity even if he does not so much as know that Jesus of Nazareth existed. And I do not think that doubts respecting the facts related in the Gospels need give us much trouble. Believing that in one way or another the thing is of God, we shall in the end know perhaps in what way and how far it was so. Trust in God's Justice, and Love, and belief in his Commands as written in our Conscience stand unshaken, though, Matthew, Mark, Luke, and John or even St Paul, were to fall.[41]

This complex mix of faith and doubt, or belief and unbelief, comes into particularly sharp focus in Clough's poem 'That there are powers above us I admit'. The poem articulates faith in one who is at once both present and absent; this happens in a split second, as the hope that Man is not alone is expressed in the claim, or non-claim that 'There *are* who walk beside us'.[42] Who they are we do not know – they are not named; we are some way from the Christian belief that there is *One* who walks beside us. The Emmaus story is again being rewritten; this time Christ does not become a blear-eyed pimp but a strangely absent

12

'who', a 'who' that are not even named as 'those'; the line, we feel, should read as 'there are *those* who walk beside us' – the pronoun 'those' seems to be missing. Christ here becomes an anonymous or even absent plural, a ghostly crowd that *are* (and *are not*) walking beside us.

A crowd, at this time, could be a potent political force. In another poem, written around 1852, Clough asks, of London's streets, 'Are the people walking quietly?'; the answer at this point was probably 'Yes', but just four years earlier things were different as, on 10 April 1848, thousands of Chartists prepared to march toward Parliament to present a petition demanding the vote for all working-class men.[43] 'There are who walk beside us' expresses a belief (or *un*belief) that is not only religious but political; Clough's (un)belief in the saving presence of God is somehow tied up with his (un)belief in the revolutionary force of the people. Critics are quick to point out that Clough, or 'Citizen Clough' as he was nicknamed in the 1840s, was a keen supporter of both Chartism at home and Republicanism abroad; less well observed is that Clough's politics are entangled with his religion. Hence Clough's spectacular cry, 'Religion, politics, O me!'[44] As early as 1838, in a letter written to Clough, J. P. Gell rages against those who are 'fixed on the personal of Christianity to the exclusion of the political'.[45] Gell has primarily in mind those evangelical believers for whom the saving of the individual soul was considered quite separate from social justice. Gell might also have in mind the Oxford Movement, which held that the Church of England was undermined or even invalidated because, as the Established Church, it was yoked to the State rather than Rome. There were, though, many around Clough for whom Christianity *was* a political affair – perhaps most obviously his Rugby headmaster, Thomas Arnold, who believed in an Established Church firmly founded on aristocratic values mediated via the newly expanded middle classes.[46] Once at Oxford, Clough himself would gravitate towards those who looked not to the rich to revive Christianity, but the poor. Though Oxford was a place of enormous wealth, Clough was exposed to abject poverty through the charitable activities of the Oxford Mendacity Society. Clough was unique amongst his circle in not just supporting the Society but actually working for it; from 1844 to

13

1848 Clough would combine his duties as a Fellow with helping at its office in the slums of St Ebbe's, where the Society sought to help the many beggars and tramps that swarmed through Oxford.[47] Clough may have had such people in mind when, in 1847, he wrote an astonishing essay on Oxford's response to the Irish famine of 1844–5. Here Clough dwells on the contrast between the privileged Christian enclave that was Oxford and the waste land that was Ireland; as Clough does so he becomes increasingly radical, until his words finally take on an almost prophetic force – drawing on New Testament parable, Clough announces: 'Many yet shall come in from the highways and hedges ... to share and share alike in our father's bequests.'[48] In 1845 J. C. Shairp writes to Clough about what he calls the 'future of Christianity'; here, Clough sees that future shaped by the poor. He seems to glimpse a thousand times over 'the ... plebeian Christian' that Dispychus sees.[49]

At the time, plebeian Christians were certainly making their presence felt. Though both Chartism and French Republicanism were largely secular movements they each contained significant religious elements. Witness the self-styled 'Chartist Chapels' whose slogan was 'Christ and universal suffrage'; note too that in the 1840s the poorest and most radical Paris revolutionaries, the so-called 'sans-culottes' (literally, 'those-without-breeches'), invoked the figure of 'Jésus sans-culottes', 'le "sans-culotte" de Nazareth', 'le Christ des barricades'.[50] For these plebeian Christians, Christ was very much on the side of the poor; to some extent, he *was* the poor man. This is very much the force of Christ's declaration, 'I was an hungred and ye gave me meat; I was thirsty and ye gave me drink ... naked and ye clothed me.'[51] Clough echoes, or even develops, this theme by merging not only Jesus and the poor man but *God* and the poor man, or God and labour:

> You have found out God have you? Why, who can it be that made all these contrivances for our comfortable existence here; who put things together for us; who built the house we live in, and the mill that we work in, and made the tools that we use; who keeps the clocks in order, and rings the bell for us, and lights the fire and cooks the victuals and lays the table for us?[52]

In just one paragraph, a question about God become a question about labour; Clough pushes aside metaphysical speculation about who God is, and confronts us instead with the more urgent question of who the workers are. For a moment it seems as if Clough actually *believes* in labour, taking it to be the source and origin of things; for a moment, he echoes the radical 1840s atheist Joseph Holyoake who talked of the 'Christ of Labour'.[53] In just the next paragraph, however, Clough seems to be as unsure as ever; as if addressing himself, he writes:

> You have found out God, have you? The vessel goes on its way: how? You conclude there is someone somewhere working these wheels, these positions, these strong and exquisitely-adapted means. Oh, my friends! and if in a dark room, under the main deck, you have hunted out a smudgy personage with a sub-intelligent look about the eyes, is that so great a gospel for me?[54]

The answer, Clough implies, is 'No', which is surprising given the influence of Carlyle's 'Gospel of Work', as evidenced in Clough's poem 'Qui laborat, orat' ('Who labours, prays').[55] It is as if when actually faced with one who labours – the 'smudgy personage with a sub-intelligent look' – Clough is not so sure.

Such wavering is echoed in the way in which Clough's socialist faith is complicated by the actual events of the French revolution of February 1848; within days of its outbreak Clough writes to Tom Arnold, 'I [do not] put much faith in Michelet's holy bayonets as preachers of any kind of Gospel.'[56] Clough's scepticism is justified when, as the bourgeoisie take control, the bayonets of the new republic are turned on the workers themselves. Clough saw these bayonets at first hand when, in May, he went to see revolutionary Paris for himself; on 19 May he writes: 'Ichabod, Ichabod, the glory is departed. Liberty, Equality, and Fraternity [is] driven back by shopkeeping bayonet.'[57] Though Clough laments what he calls this 'Bourgeoisistic triumph', he also acknowledges, and even plays up, his own position as a detached, bourgeois observer of events: 'I do little else than potter about under the Tuileries Chestnuts ...', 'the perpetual gunfire [gives] ... me a headache'.[58] This ironic distance is replayed in *Amours de Voyage* where Clough presents a parody of himself in the effete figure of Claude, the love-sick tourist who, when caught in the very middle of the 1848 siege of

Rome, only notices that the fighting has begun because the café has no milk for his coffee. Clough's ironic point is that 'there are who walk beside us', or even fight and die beside us, *but that is not to say we shall necessarily notice*. This is, in part, the gist of 'there are who walk beside us' which, with the missing word 'those', is as much about absence as presence. It is a curious feature of Clough's streets that one can walk beside someone, or in parallel with them, without actually meeting them. In 'Sic Itur', in a strange and almost geometric vision of parallel lines, Clough imagines two men 'who take one street's two sides', but even though they 'walk one way' 'each to the other goes unseen'.[59] The same may be said of Clough and the blear-eyed pimp who 'beside me walked' on Easter Day; even this street-walking Christ is as much absent as present – he is mentioned just once.

Citizen Clough takes not only faith onto the streets but also doubt; Clough's doubter, we recall, is like one who 'standeth still i' the *street*'. In this he is unusual; most middle-class Victorians tended to do their doubting indoors, in the private space that was the drawing-room, the library, the college, or even the church. It is true that Charles Darwin goes to sea for six years as a young man and publishes widely, but once he has done so he increasingly shuts himself away with his family.[60] It is also true that Matthew Arnold, in his poem 'Dover Beach', goes to the coast to doubt and even looks across to France, but he ends the poem alone with his wife: 'Ah love, let us be true/ To one another!'[61] Such domestic retreat is not, though, for the doubting Clough; not simply because he does not marry until he is 35, but also because he wants to see what doubt might mean 'out there', amongst the people, on the streets. Darwin, like many of his class, feared it could only mean a terrible revolution; a fear reflected in the substantial number of working-class atheists who were tried and imprisoned for blasphemy in the 1840s. This is very much the argument of Ross Marsh who points out that, whilst middle-class expressions of doubt were often tolerated, the mere idea of working-class atheism, or mass unbelief, was quite terrifying.[62] For Clough, the idea was far from terrifying. Witness the growing excitement as, in 'Easter Day', he imagines a whole city learning to doubt:

As circulates in some great city crowd
A rumour changeful, vague, importunate, and loud,
From no determined centre, or of fact,
    Or authorship exact,
    Which no man can deny
    Nor verify;
    So spread the wondrous fame;
    …
    He was not risen, no,
      Christ was not risen![63]

In Oxford, Clough imagines himself standing still in the street, a lone doubter; here in Naples he imagines street after street positively crowded with doubters. Suddenly, doubt is not a solitary and frozen state but a dynamic and popular movement; it is as if the one who asks 'why should I …dance about to music that I hear not?' is joined by everyone, as if *no one* can now hear the music to which they are dancing. And that is precisely what Clough sees in revolutionary Paris; writing to Stanley in May 1848, Clough describes how a festival is called to celebrate the new republic and how, with the whole of the Champs Élysées decorated like 'a great ball room', many were 'dancing vigorously' – but 'dancing', adds Clough, *'without music'.*[64]

This strange and poignant vision is, in part, the jaundiced vision of one who is convinced that the new, bourgeois Republic is no longer dancing to any real, revolutionary music; it is, in this sense, a scene of collective delusion. But at least the delusion is collective, at least each dancer could say 'there are who *dance* beside us'. Clough's Parisian scene is a scene of strange faith – the strange faith that the unhearing doubter is not alone, that *no one* can hear the music and indeed that, in dancing as if they did, the music is almost *danced* into existence.

NOT

Our business is *not* … to 'stand still'.[65]

        (Francis Newman to Clough, 6 December 1847)

Clough knows well what dance makes possible. Having asked 'Why should I dance about to music that I hear not?' Clough initially comforts himself with the hope that one day he *will*

17

hear, that 'yet anon [I] shall hear'; but until that happens, 'till that arrive', his soul must its own 'music make', and to do this he is to 'keep amid the throng,/ And turn as they shall turn, and bound as they are bounding'.[66] There is a part of Clough that cannot resist dancing; as Dipsychus puts it, 'stand out the waltz … Is it possible?' – is it possible *not* to hope that dancing will the 'music make'?[67] This hope is encoded in the 1851 poem 'Dance on, dance on, we see, we see', which almost becomes 'we hear, we hear', as Clough cries,

> Wind, wind your waltzes, wind and wheel,
> Our senses too with *music reel*.[68]

For 'music reel' we cannot but read, or hear, 'music *real*'. Clough certainly entertains the possibility of a music that is real enough to continue even after our dancing has stopped; as he writes to his sister Anne in November 1848,

> If *we* die and come to nothing, it does not therefore follow that Life and goodness will cease to be in Earth and Heaven. If we give over dancing, it does not therefore follow that the dance ceases itself, *or the Music*.[69]

Clough believes in the 'Music' of a 'Life and goodness' that exists beyond the limits of individual life; this 'Life' is not the transcendental Christian God but a variation on that conventional theme. Much the same may be said of Clough's music; that too is unfamiliar, or unconventional. For Clough, there are 'two musics': one is 'loud and bold … All tone and tune' – this, though, is not Clough's music; the other, the music Clough *does* hear, is

> … soft and low
> Stealing whence we not know,
> Painfully heard, and easily forgot,
> With pauses oft and many a silence strange,
> (And silent oft it seems, when silent it is not)
> …
> Listen, listen, listen, – is it not sounding now?[70]

As Clough strains to hear silent-seeming music he is mindful of the Greek concept of the music of the spheres, that music produced by the movement of the heavens which was so beautiful as to be inaudible. This is the music John Keats

18

famously hears, or rather does not hear: 'Heard melodies are sweet, but those unheard/ Are sweeter.'[71] There is, though, nothing sweet, or even beautiful about the spiritual music of Clough's world – moving in and out of silence, this music is fitful, 'strange', and even 'painfully heard'. Clough, it seems, is not so much looking (or listening) back to the ancient music of the spheres but rather attempting to describe a self-consciously modern music, a music of the spirit that is appropriate to the 1840s, to a decade of question, doubt, hunger and revolution. If so, he is peculiarly successful since, in exactly the same year as Clough published 'Why should I', Kierkegaard was writing about 'the strange acoustics of the life of spirit'.[72] Kierkegaard says no more about these strange acoustics, or the music they may produce, but Clough does; indeed, his talk of a spiritual music that is strange, fitful and 'painfully heard' seems to us *now* as not just modern but modern*ist*, almost anticipating the atonal music of the early twentieth century. At the same time as Clough chances upon the 'future of Christianity', so he chances upon the future of music. This seems to happen again when Dipsychus, the double-minded doubter who cannot decide on the existence of God, declares that anyone who decides prematurely is like one who would dance 'while the instruments are [still] tuning'.[73] The image is striking, even absurd; for Dipsychus, to believe is like trying to dance to the discord, or disharmony that one day will come to dominate modernist music. Dipsychus can already hear the painful discord of the post-Christian era, the painful music of the God-less spheres:

> I dreamt a dream; till morning light
> A bell rang in my head all night,
> Tinkling and tinkling first, and then
> Tolling; and tinkling; tolling again.
> So brisk and gay, and then so slow!
> O joy, and terror! mirth and woe!
> Ting, ting, there is no God; ting, ting –
> Dong, there is no God; dong,
> ...
> Ting, ting ... [74]

In the middle of the nineteenth century the acoustics of the spirit do indeed appear to be strange, if not absurd. 'Listen, listen, listen,' says Clough; however, when, as Dipsychus,

19

Clough finally does hear the music ('ting, ting –/ Dong, there is no God; dong') it is almost too painful, too awful. Clough seems ready for this; having initially strained to 'listen, listen, listen', Clough goes on, curiously, to declare: 'may the ear ... *not* hear'.[75] This is a difficult and contradictory poem that does, at times, seem to believe in some kind of music of the spirit; at the end, however, Clough suddenly seems to discard music, and dream simply of spirit, or soul – his final desire is that

> ... the bare conscience of the better thing
> Unfelt, unseen, unimaged, all unknown,
> May fix the entranced soul ...

This dream of 'bare conscience', or pure knowledge ('con-science' here meaning 'inward knowledge') implies that music, like any other image or representation, merely gets in the way of God, or 'the better thing'. For Clough, this better thing can only be encountered, or 'conscience[d]' in the *absence* of image, whether that image be visual or aural. With iconoclastic zeal, Clough here assaults the traditional conviction that music might reflect, or somehow re-present, God.

This he does again in 'Adam and Eve', where Adam accuses Eve of having 'some religious *crotchet* in your head'; even in Eden there is no religious *music* – instead, only religious *notation*.[76] Music cannot give us God; all it can do is offer merely arbitrary, man-made signs and codes that are no more like God than a crotchet is like the note that is actually played. In a single phrase, Clough's Adam has come close to such sceptical Victorian philosophers of language as Carlyle, Sir William Hamilton, and H. L. Mansel – thinkers whom W. David Shaw has called 'agnostic semioticians', since their fear that no words could ever denote God extended to a more general, semiotic suspicion of the capacity of language to mirror or represent anything.[77] Like most of his generation, Clough was thoroughly versed in Carlyle and, as Shaw points out, Clough would certainly have been aware of the philosophical agnosticism of Hamilton, if only via the scepticism of his Oxford tutor W. G. Ward and the radical uncertainty of his friend Matthew Arnold.[78] Shaw sees in Arnold 'the loneliness of the quester who seeks univocal [unproblematic] discourse with God ... but who is left in the end with only blank counters and extrinsic signs' – religious crotchets rather than religious music, as it were.[79]

For Clough's Adam, the crotchet is, as he tells Eve, 'in your head' – a bald and almost bathetic phrase that echoes Dipsychus's equally bathetic 'in my head': the bell that went 'Dong, there is no God' rang 'in my head'.[80] Clough is strangely insistent that what is left of God is a mental event: his 'God ... was *thought*-of still'; all that we have left of God is the thought of God. This familiar idea turns unfamiliar in 'Cease, empty Faith', where we read: 'I, God, am nought: a shade of thought.' Here Clough's thinking about God takes the form of God himself thinking; momentarily we encounter not so much the thought *of* God but the thought of *God*: 'I, God, am.'[81] Paradoxically, the encounter takes place even as God is declaring himself to be no more than 'a *shade* of thought'. This echoes the latest theology with its claim that God is a mere shade, or shadow, of the human mind. Expressed here as God-equals-shadow, the new theology reads like Plato in reverse – Plato, the Greek philosopher, held that the human world is the shadow of which God is the substance.[82]

Plato makes another, more obvious appearance (this time the right way round) in the poem 'Uranus', where Clough has 'Plato in me', saying: 'Mind not the stars, mind thou thy Mind and God.'[83] As Plato argues in *The Republic*, God is not to be known through thinking about the world (not even the stars) but rather through thinking itself; in Clough, the human mind is thus capitalized as 'Mind' – on a par, it seems, with 'God'.[84] It is as if Clough expects to find not only 'Plato in me' but '*God* in me'. And that, in a sense, is what happens when Clough ventrilo-quizes: 'I, God, am'; it is, though, astonishingly: 'I, God, am *nought*.' 'God in me' somehow announces his own non-being. The God of thought is a vulnerable God.

And so he is, or was. Nineteenth-century accounts of God-as-thought were dominated by Hegel who argued that God, or (as Hegel himself would say) Spirit or Mind (*Geist*), is still in process – a process that entails negation, even the negation of death:

God has died – God is dead – this is the most frightful of all thought ... that Negation itself is found in God.[85]

21

This seems to be echoed in 'I, God, am nought'; the echo might just be deliberate, Clough was well aware of Hegel.[86] What makes, though, the moment of negation so different in Clough is that it is somehow imagined from within, from God's own perspective. For a split second, the grandly objective drama of Hegelian world history becomes a merely subjective drama, the drama of an I, or self. This too reflects Victorian philosophy, where Hegel's Absolute Idealism often shaded into the Personal Idealism of such as F. C. S. Schiller and A. S. Pringle-Pattison. We are again in territory marked out by W. David Shaw, who argues that such high philosophy was part of a far wider movement in Victorian culture:

> When Pringle-Pattison turns Hegel's doctrine of absolute or eternal self-making from a statement about God into a statement about man, he fosters the existential notion that Victorian man is not just a maker but self-maker ... Such a notion pervades the verse of ... Clough.[87]

This is clear in 'The New Sinai', where we are told:

> ... ah, wait in faith
> God's self-completing plan;
> Receive it not, but leave it not,
> And wait it out, O man![88]

Told neither to receive God's plan nor to leave it, Man is left to wait – left to make up his own plan, a plan that is, therefore, 'self-completing' in the sense of not only completing itself but of completing the self, or at least of attempting to do so.

One who struggles to complete himself is Clough's fallen Adam; separated from God in the world outside Eden, Adam talks of 'A wakeful, changeless touchstone in my brain,/ Receiving, noting, testing all the while/ These passing, curious, new phenomena.'[89] Adam concludes by declaring 'Myself my own experiment'. For 'fallen Adam' read 'Victorian man'; both see the question of God fast turning into the question of self, or me. In *Amours de Voyages* Mary Trevellyn speaks better than she knows when asking, 'Is it religion? I ask me.'[90]

Shaw is clearly right in saying that existential notions pervade Clough's verse and, in particular, that Clough's Adam is a 'proto-existentialist'.[91] We must, though, be careful since full-blown Existentialism, the French Existentialism of the late 1940s and

22

1950s, is thoroughly atheist; according to Jean-Paul Sartre and Albert Camus, Man must constantly make himself in an absolutely God-less void. In contrast, Clough's Adam allows some space for God: though Adam is 'parted' from God, he is addressing him ('O thou God') even as he declares 'Myself my own experiment'.[92] Adam is proto-existential in much the same way as Søren Kierkegaard was. In 1849, the very same year that Clough has Adam alone and self-experimental before God, Kierkegaard publishes *Sickness Unto Death* in which he writes of 'the self ... whose task is to become itself' but adds that this 'can only be done in the relationship to God'.[93] It has long been acknowledged that Kierkegaard's agonized, Protestant self provides Existentialism with a Christian pre-history. If, then, we speak of Clough as a proto-existentialist we must remember that, for all his agnosticism, Clough is part of a pre-history to Existentialism that is still Christian. For Kierkegaard, 'to risk unreservedly being oneself' is what he calls 'Christian hero-ism'.[94] When Adam makes himself his own experiment outside Eden, or indeed when Clough risks unreservedly being himself outside Oxford, they are (though they do not know it) heroic Kierkegaardian Christians.

Clough would never have read Kierkegaard, whose work was scarcely known outside of Denmark; Clough was, though, a good friend of Florence Nightingale, who as well as being a Crimean nurse, wrote extensively on philosophical and theological themes – in particular on what she calls 'this anxious existence'.[95] Nightingale never gets a mention in the histories, or pre-histories of Existentialism, and only rarely is she mentioned in relation to Clough, but in her privately printed *Suggestions for Thought* (a book she discussed with Clough) there are moments which suggest she is important in both respects. This astonishing book includes the propositions that 'God is developing himself' and that 'God thinks at one time and not at another'.[96] These are propositions Nightingale goes on to dispute, but they are genuinely striking in the way they articulate an almost Hegelian sense of a God-in-process, a God responsible for his own self-making – in short, a God who looks like the Kierkegaardian hero. When Nightingale talks of putting 'the whole relation between God and man ... upon the footing of responsibility' it is almost as if she *had* somehow read Kierkegaard.[97]

The same might be said of another writer whose work was well known to Clough – namely, Francis Newman. In his review of Newman's book *The Soul*, Clough describes Newman's internalized Christianity, and particularly its claim that 'the Kingdom of God is within us', as 'something of a religious ontology'.[98] Newman, implies Clough, has an almost religious belief in human being – or, more precisely, in individual human being. So too does Newman's brother, John Henry, the Catholic convert; ironically, he gets even closer to Kierkegaard's hyper-Protestant stress on the *being* of the individual believer:

> If I am asked why I believe in a God, I answer that it is because I believe in Myself, for I feel it impossible to believe in my own existence (and of that I am quite sure) without believing also in the existence of Him who lives as an All-seeing, All-Judging Being in my conscience.[99]

The problem for Clough is that he is not so sure of his own existence, or rather is aware that human being is not so much a fact as a question or riddle; our fate, he declares, is

> To spend uncounted years of pain,
> Again, again, and yet again,
> In working out in heart and brain
> The problem of our being here.[100]

This problem is only heightened when it is entangled with the problem of God. We return to Clough's primary question: 'Why should I say I see the things I see not,/ *Why be and be not?*' For Hamlet, the question is: 'To be or not to be'; here that question becomes the still more difficult question of 'why be *and* be not'.

EX

> Cross-currents we have ... this is the River of Existence.
>
> (Thomas Carlyle, 1833)[101]

To be *and* be not is to inhabit two mutually exclusive states; for Clough, being seems to be an almost impossible trick, one beyond mere mortals. And so it seems in Clough's poem 'The Angel', where the task of existence, of being-in-the-world, is assigned to an unnamed angel:

Exist – come forth –
O Phantom, in the Almighty name of God
And in his Power, his delegate for this,
Exist, come forth, I bid thee, Seem to be.

Go and perform his mission there below
Go – and as some ill-omened bird of night
Half-bird, half-beast, with foul and dismal way
Hover and flit about this human soul
Flapping thy black temptation in his face
While the time, his time and thine – Exist.[102]

For this angel, this 'delegate' of God, to exist is an extreme act of
extreme will. Merely by existing, the angel runs the risk of not
existing; it is already a 'Phantom', as if already half-dead. The 'ex'
in exist (particularly the second 'exist') suggests the 'ex' that
means 'no more'. To choose to be vulnerable, to choose to risk not
being, may seem a strange way to exist 'in the Almighty name of
God', but then, for the Victorians, God is quite capable of
choosing to die. This was particularly true of *believing* Victorians
who understood that God, as Christ, chose not only to be mortal
but to provoke the religious authorities; He thus chose, twice-
over, to die. Much the same idea is also on the mind of those
*un*believing Victorians who, like Clough, were beginning to talk
of 'God's death', a conceit that begs the question: 'Who killed
him?' For Nietzsche, in 1888, the terrible and wonderful answer is
that *we* did, that '*We* have killed him'; for the mid-Victorians,
however, it is thinkable that God is his own murderer, that he
chooses to die.[103] In 1870, when Swinburne imagines the first line
of a blasphemous newspaper report on God's death, he comes up
with 'Suicide of an elderly pauper lunatic'.[104] Though Clough is
never so crude, when he writes that 'sure, slow poisons wrought
God's death's work' we cannot escape the thought that God took
the poison himself, that (to mis-read ever so slightly) the poisons
are God's work. In a poem written a few years before, in 1830,
Clough writes: 'Well I mind me of the day when Socrates was
tried' – the Greek philosopher Socrates was condemned to die by
drinking poison;[105] God's death-by-poison thus reminds us of the
day when Socrates died, died at his own hands. In Clough, 'God's
death' speaks of God's freedom, his capacity to choose. Today's
reader might think God is, self-evidently, free to choose, but
Clough's friend Nightingale was adamant that 'God … has no

freewill' since, she argued, he 'cannot choose ... evil'.[106] This familiar theological argument is countered when the Spirit in *Dipsychus* declares that 'God can act the Devil when He chooses'.[107] If God can *choose* to play the devil, he can also choose to die.

Clough is certainly preoccupied with the *man* who chooses to die – namely, the martyr. The effete Claude may not be rushing to enlist as one – 'I 'list not ... for the glorious army of martyrs!' – but Clough himself *is* drawn to the martyr, or at least what he intriguingly calls the 'half martyr'.[108] Clough strains to hear 'the sigh, wherein a martyr's breath/ Exhales from ignominious death/ For some lost cause!'[109] Just two months after publishing this 'sigh' Clough does himself get to play the martyr as he resigns his fellowship at Oxford, a place that Arnold would soon famously call the '*home* of lost causes'.[110] The martyr who dies for 'some lost cause' is code for an Oxford martyr, or at least the Cloughean half-martyr. Oxford, we must remember, had a history of producing martyrs – most famously, the Protestant reformers Cranmer, Latimer and Ridley, all of whom were, in the 1550s, burnt for heresy outside Balliol, Clough's own college. There is no doubt that the shadow of these burnings falls across the ferocious religious debates of 1840s Oxford. Referring to the university's formal 'degradation' of Clough's Tractarian tutor, W. G. Ward, Stanley once wrote:

> Had it been the sixteenth, instead of the nineteenth, century, just the same men, with just the same arguments, would have been voting not for degradation, but for burning.[111]

A similar thought is in the mind of Froude, whose controversial novel of religious doubt, *The Nemesis of Faith*, was publicly burnt in February 1849 by the rector of Exeter College, Oxford; writing to Clough, Froude makes it clear that he feels as if he himself is being burnt: 'Oxford grows rapidly too hot for me ... I was *preached* against ... in Chapel ... and yesterday *burnt* publicly.'[112]

Six years before, Gell writes to Clough, 'you seem to be in the midst of the Oxford heresies'.[113] Gell speaks better than he intends, for the word 'heretic' (as both he and Clough would know well) comes from the Greek *hairetikos* meaning 'able to choose'; the Oxford heretic is able to choose, but this privilege comes at the cost of burning. For Clough, the man who is able to choose is doomed to live in a crucible; Clough's Adam, he who calls 'myself my own experiment', immediately prefaces this with, 'tortured in the crucible I lie'.[114] Clough's almost twentieth-century vision of the experimental self is combined with an almost sixteenth-century vision of torture-by-fire. It is clear, for Clough, that freedom is a terrible thing, curse rather than privilege. This is precisely how Existentialists would come to see freedom; according to Sartre, writing in 1940s Paris, 'man is *condemned* to be free'.[115] Clough knows and lives this a hundred years before, in 1840s Oxford, a place where man is free to be condemned, condemned to a kind of burning.

This fate finds cryptic expression when, in 'Ah, what is love', Clough talks of what remains when love is gone; echoing the 'Ah' that begins the poem, Clough sighs:

> ... Ah me,
> Go look in little space,
> White ash on blackened earth will be
> Sole record of its place.[116]

Here, in just nine words, the poem moves from 'Ah' to 'ash'. Has 'AH' himself, *A. H.* Clough, been through fire? Karl Marx would certainly expect as much; writing just a few years later, and glancing at the humanistic re-interpretation of Christianity particularly associated with the German theologian Ludwig *Feuerbach* (literally 'stream of fire'), Marx punningly proclaims: 'Christians ... there is no other road for you to truth ... except that leading through the stream of fire.'[117] Clough does seem to have taken Marx's advice. Just four years before 'Ah, what is love', Clough concluded another poem with the bold declaration: 'I remain A.H.C.';[118] Clough, though, has *not* remained AHC. For now 'I ... A.H.C.' is humbled, or reduced to a plain and desperate 'Ah me' – 'I' has become 'me' and 'AHC' has become just 'Ah'. And, as we know, 'Ah' in turn becomes mere 'ash'.

'*White* ash on *black*ened earth' is an inverted form of writing – the usual black on white becoming white on black. Clough, the 'inverse Saul', here dreams of inverse writing; it is a strange dream of strange writing. And such writing is to become central to Clough's account of true religion, or at least true soul. In 1850, Clough declares that

27

> On the rock of the human soul stands the mystic inscription, the characters of the strange alphabet ... Variable, shifting, now this, now that, Egyptian, Chaldean, Etruscan, Assyrian.[119]

The strange alphabet of Clough's soul is so strange that elsewhere it is not so much a case of 'now this, now that' but 'now this *and* that'. In *Dipsychus*, in parody of symbolic logic, the Spirit declares, 'we cannot act without assuming x,/ And at the same time y'.[120] Five years before, when raging against Oxford's dogmatic interpretation of the Thirty-Nine Articles, Clough asks, 'What right have our MAs to say whether statements x, y, z agree or not with the Articles?'[121] Clough's implication is that often x, y and z can be said to both agree and not agree. This is the force of 'Why be *and* be not?' which, in this connection, can be reread as 'why b and b not?' When it comes to the question of faith, Clough is for ever, as he himself remarks, 'dreadfully double-minded'; as many have observed, Clough *is* Dipsychus (literally, 'double-souled').[122] What has not been observed is that, in Clough, double-mindedness finds almost algebraic expression – no surprise given that Clough's studies included both Logic and Mathematics. For Clough, we might say, you can have x and y at the same time, you can (or must) b and b not. This is the strange self-cancelling algebra of agnosticism; and what makes it still more strange is that it points towards a self-cancelling form of writing, a form of writing that is also a form of unwriting, or anti-writing.

Glimpses of such writing are frequent and conspicuous in Clough; as we might expect from this double-spirited, dialectical poet for whom, like Marx, 'everything seems pregnant with its contrary'. As Clough puts it, 'the plot has counterplot.'[123] Hence his talk of 'weaving and unweaving, learning and unlearning', 'thinkings and cross-thinkings', even 'crossings and counter-crossings'.[124] This last refers to the act of writing and is echoed when Clough declares:

> If to write, rewrite, and write again,
> Bite now the lip and now the pen,
> ...
> Inside and out turn a phrase, o'er and o'er,
> Till all the little sense goes, it had before, –
> ...
> If it be these things that make one a poet,
> I am one ...[125]

Writing and rewriting 'till all the little sense goes', Clough ends with less than he began. For Clough, to write is to rewrite, and to rewrite is to *un*write. This riddle certainly makes philosophical sense; elsewhere, Clough echoes the traditional, Platonic condemnation of writing as something *less* than thought: 'by writing', he declares, 'we unlearn' – '*The Iliad* is but the scum of the mind of Homer, and Plato's [written] dialogues the refuse of his thought.'[126] Literary and philosophical tradition clearly gives Clough sufficient cause to be wary of writing; there is, though, good autobiographical cause in that the central drama, or trauma, of his life is an act of unwriting – the resignation of his Oriel fellowship. On 12 October 1848, Clough writes to E. A. Hawkins, the Master of Oriel:

> I must ... beg you to submit to the College my ... paper of resignation ... *Ego Arturus Hugo Clough* ... resigno.[127]

Clough signs the paper, 'A. H. Clough'; in doing so, he simply does as requested by Hawkins:

> I send the ... form of Resignation, which should be signed and sent to me.[128]

Here, to sign is also to unsign, to cancel the Oriel fellowship. 'To write, rewrite and write again ... till all the little sense goes' is a paradox that Clough lives out. He thus arrives at the paradox of writing via the paradox of the *signature*. In so doing, Clough anticipates Jacques Derrida for whom, as Derek Attridge puts it, 'the function of the signature in our legal culture is dependent upon two contradictory properties, its unique affirmation of the here-and-now of the signatory, and its repeatability ... [or] reproducibility'.[129] Clough does not problematize the signature in any such philosophical way, but he does sense or feel an acute problem. When Gell pleads, 'pray why not sign the XXXIX Articles, you must sign something', Clough explains that his reluctance in doing so is

> not so much from any definite objection to this or that point as [a] general dislike to Subscription and strong feeling of its being ... a bondage, and very heavy one, and one that may cramp one and cripple one for life.[130]

For Clough, the problem of the signature is almost pathological – to sign, he feels, would entail an acute and recurring physical handicap, or burden; it would be (to echo the proverb) a cross to bear.[131] Indeed, Clough's problem with signing the articles of faith is haunted by the central sign, or signature of that faith – namely, the Cross.

Clough, we must remember, is operating within a culture where the Cross is fast becoming a difficult and problematic sign. Not only were many ceasing to believe at all but even amongst those who did there was a general shift from a theology of Atonement, with its focus on the death of Christ, to a theology of Incarnation, with its focus on the life of Christ.[132]No wonder Arnold should cry, 'Leave ... the Cross', Swinburne declare, 'the Cross ... creak[s]', and Charlotte Brontë see it as a 'dusky sign'. When Dickens writes, of revolutionary Paris, that 'the sign of ... the Cross was discarded and denied', it is clear that he is also writing about Victorian London – in *Bleak House* 'the great cross on the summit of St Paul's Cathedral' is London's 'crowning confusion'.[133] If Dickens is right, the sign of the Cross has become the sign of confusion; it is not just a problematic sign but a sign of the problem with all signs, all meanings. It is no surprise that Carlyle's critique of signs and symbols should climax with the Cross:

> Nay, the highest ensign that men ever met under and embraced under, the Cross itself, had no meaning save an accidental extrinsic one.[134]

When Clough writes of 'thinkings and cross-thinkings', 'crossings and counter-crossings' we are not far from Carlyle's crossed-out Cross, the Cross that is merely a sign, an accidental and alterable mark.

For the *young* Clough, the Cross is a fact of history. It is also a fact of his own spiritual life: drawing on standard evangelical theology, the undergraduate Clough declares that his sins have 'crucified [Christ] afresh & afresh'.[135] In so doing, Clough gives an account of the Cross that anticipates Derrida's account of the signature; like Derrida's signature, Clough's Cross is at once both unique (a crucifixion of Christ 'afresh') and yet also repeatable ('afresh *and* afresh'). The result is that the Cross can no longer be mistaken for a simple historical fact, or event; by 1852, Clough confesses, 'whether Christ died upon the cross, I cannot tell'.[136] The course of Clough's changing beliefs thus tells

30

of an all-too-repeatable Cross that increasingly leads the strange life of a sign, unfixed and free. The same story is told by the poem 'Easter Day' with its sceptical talk of 'an after-Gospel', a rewriting of the Cross that is so free as to include the Resurrection.[137] As Joe Phelan notes, 'after-Gospel' is a reference to the late dating given to the Christian Gospels by the new German theologians; each of the four Gospels, Clough implies, is an after-Gospel, a belated writing and rewriting of the Cross until 'all the little sense goes'.[138] Here the after-Gospel appears to be a lesser gospel.

Things, though, are not so simple; for Clough himself writes an after-Gospel. This is the poem that comes *after* 'Easter Day' – namely, 'Easter Day II', which makes possible, or thinkable, an 'Easter Day III', 'Easter Day IV' and so on.[139] Suddenly, Easter cannot stop, it has a future. Clough, as we know, was mindful of 'the future of Christianity'; so too was Nightingale with her talk of 'the next Christ', and Tennyson in *In Memoriam* with his talk of 'the Christ that is to be'.[140] Nightingale believes that 'the next Christ will perhaps be a female Christ', and Tennyson that 'the Christ that is to be' will resemble Arthur Hallam; Clough, though, has no clear belief. The nearest he comes to any prophecy is in his 1847 essay on Oxford's response to the Irish Famine; here Clough envisages a future in which both the material and spiritual privileges of Christian Oxford will be shared: 'many yet shall come in from the highways and hedges, and join in the meal with us that came early'. So far, so biblical – Clough is echoing New Testament parable; however, he goes on, in strange and cryptic fashion, to predict that:

> a posthumous brother is yet to be born, to share and share alike in our father's bequests.[141]

In Clough's after-Gospel, all we know about the one who is to come is that he will be a 'posthumous' child – in other words, he will only be born once 'our father' is dead. Clough has given us a cryptogram of the death of God. Indeed, given that the posthumous child, or brother comes in from the highways and hedges of famine-stricken Ireland, where one million have starved to death, we here glimpse the possibility of the death of God being repeated a million times. For Clough, the death of

31

God is an event that, like Derrida's signature, is necessarily repeatable. It is, therefore, not yet finished.

This is the gist of that almost interminable line, 'the slow sure poisons [that] wrought God's death's work, God's doom'. Here Clough writes and rewrites the Hegelian 'death of God' as death after death after death in a potentially infinite series. In doing so, Clough turns a classic statement of doubt into a statement of faith, faith in God's absolute identification with the unique and yet all-too-repeatable event that is human death. This, Clough implies, is 'God's death's work' – the work of God's death.

It is work that exhausts both language and logic: 'slow sure poisons [that] wrought God's death's work, God's doom' is a line that pushes syntax to breaking point and thought to the absolute limit. By the line's end we feel that 'all the little sense has gone', and that we are left only with big sense, sense too big for words. God's death thus takes us to the threshold of silence. But then silence, for Clough, is revelation, is what he wants, paradoxically, to say:

> There is a religion whose revelation it is to be what religion so-called calls irreligion. It is, shall we *say*, Silence.[142]

2

A Man Killed: The Thought of History

WHAT

> What! ...
> Armies ... bleed; cities burn...
> ...
> What!...
> ... die mistaken ...?
>
> *(The Bothie)*
>
> What! shall the nation wait?
>
> ('Dipsychus Continued')[1]

For Clough, the thought of history always comes as something of a shock; we live, he insists, 'amid the shocks of time'.[2] Bleeding armies, burning cities, and waiting nations thus provoke not a questioning 'What?' but the exclamatory 'What!' Customarily, the word 'what' ushers in a question, most famously the philosopher's question 'What *is*?' – for example, 'What is Enlightenment?' (Immanuel Kant), 'What is Literature ? (Jean-Paul Sartre) and, indeed, 'What is History?' (E. H. Carr).[3] In Clough, the word 'what' does the very different, almost *anti*-philosophical work of exclamation. Tolstoy writes about the 'question of history' and Marx 'the *riddle* of history', but in Clough, who saw history for himself – first in revolutionary Paris and then in besieged Rome – history has little or nothing to do with the philosophical world of question and answer, riddle and solution.[4]

This makes Clough very unusual in early-Victorian England, a culture that thought of itself as part of 'the enquiring age' in which the central enquiry was, to quote Carlyle, 'Whence came

33

it, and Why and How?'[5] If Reason was the master term for the mid-eighteenth century, and Imagination was central for the Romantics, for the early Victorians it was History that was beginning to take centre stage – for many, it was fast becoming *the* form of knowledge, *the* way to interrogate the world. Writing in 1830, Carlyle declares that 'all learners, all enquiring minds of every order, are gathered round … [History's] footstool'.[6] This view was echoed by one who sat on that footstool – namely, Clough's headmaster Thomas Arnold who, from 1841, sat upon the Regius Chair of History at Oxford, a post that in itself reflects the gradual emergence of History as part of establishment culture. Soon histories seem to be everywhere; in the late fifties Clough's letters refer to a whole number of histories – from Froude's *History of England*, through Carlyle's *Frederick the Great*, to Buckle's *History of Civilisation*.[7] For Clough, though, history is not so much established as *dis*established, if only because it has so little to do with civilization. Soon after committing the world's first ever murder, Clough's Cain sees a future of 'slaughter on slaughter'; as Cain himself asks, 'This is … history then … is it?'[8] Cain puts the question of history but not quite as Tolstoy does; Cain's is a questioning *of* history, a questioning that implies not the greatness of history but the littleness, not how much it explains but how little. Cain follows his talk of 'slaughter on slaughter' with the devastating rhetorical question, 'And all for what?'

Cain's 'what?' expects no answer. In expressing astonishment at the sheer illogic of history, it echoes the 'what!' with which Adam expresses *his* astonishment at the illogic of the Fall: 'What! Because I plucked an apple from a twig!' History, it seems, begins with a shock; and, for Clough and the Oxford establishment, history begins with the shock of 1848. This was not only the year of Clough's infamous resignation and Parliament's approval of the Oxford Commission, but also the year of the Chartists' mass demonstration on Kennington Common and a whole series of violent revolutions right across Europe. As Mark Pattison recalled in 1883, 'if any Oxford man had gone to sleep in 1846 and had woken up again in 1850 he would have found himself in a totally new world'.[9] In the twentieth century James Joyce would declare that 'History … is a nightmare from which I am trying to awake', but in 1848 England (or rather a certain

Oxonian England) awakes *to* the nightmare of history.[10] Thirty-three years had passed since Wellington's defeat of Napoleon at Waterloo, thirty-three years of relative peace, quite long enough for what Clough calls the 'insular ... English' to succumb to 'a dream/ Of England'.[11] It was a dream from which, Clough adds, 'I woke' – and so too did England; but then, it had little choice with the French revolution of 1848 renewing the fear of invasion: in 1853 Frederick Temple writes to Clough, 'if Louis Nap. [*sic*] comes he will not find us asleep'.[12]

Louis Napoleon does not come – there was no invasion, not even an attempt at one; in England the shock of 1848 was the very peculiar shock of history at one remove. And it is this very complex shock that often concerns Clough. Witness *The Bothie,* where Clough's leisured Oxford undergraduates clearly do not know the shock of actually going to war, but do know the shock of merely the thought: after talking of bleeding armies and burning, Philip exclaims: 'What! would ourselves for the cause of an hour encounter the battle,/ Slay and be slain ...?'[13] War does get closer in *Amours de Voyage* where Claude *et al.* find themselves caught in the middle of the siege of Rome; here, though, what shocks is not so much the witnessing of history as the *thought* of witnessing history: 'Only *think,* dearest Louisa, what fearful scenes we have witnessed!'[14]

As Clough's characters get closer to history, so they somehow retreat or recoil; merely witnessing history is a shock they cannot get over. But then, for Clough, witnessing history is itself a historical experience; as Claude exclaims at the very height of the siege,

So, I have seen a man killed! An experience that, among others![15]

It is, though, an experience that, in quite astonishing fashion, completely unravels even as Claude attempts to describe it:

Yes, I suppose I have; although I can hardly be certain,
And in a court of justice could never declare I had seen it.
But a man was killed, I am told, in a place where I saw
Something; a man was killed, I am told, and I saw something.

In just five lines 'I saw a man killed' is reduced to 'I saw something'; the very stuff of so much history (namely, killing) all but vanishes in the act of telling, or interpreting. Claude here comes close to Nietzsche – writing thirty years later, the German philosopher would insist that the French Revolution was interpreted for so long and so passionately that it became 'the text [which] disappeared under ... interpretation'.[16] Carlyle is onto something similar when, in 1833, he writes of how 'any History ... in rapidest law of perspective ... dwindles from the canvas!'[17] For Clough, though, the canvas or text of history does not quite dwindle to nothing, does not quite disappear – there is at least something left: 'I saw/ Something,' says Claude, 'I saw something.' In Clough, something is left of history. In his final, unfinished poem 'Mari Magno', Clough writes of 'a something that refuses to be stirred' – he adds, 'the petals of today,/ To-morrow fallen away,/ Shall something leave instead'.[18] The same poem also looks back to a revolutionary France and, to illustrate how 'actions ... are easily forgot', relates the story of the conseil who 'in the [year of] *quarante-huite* had something done/ ... some notice should have won'.[19] For Clough, though, the 'something' that is left of history is not simply a memory, or residue, 'a something that refuses to be stirred'; it is also a something that promises radical change: in 'Mari Magno' the Clergyman sonorously announces, 'Something there is ... *bent on revolution.*'[20]

What is left after Claude's long and anxious interpretation is, then, a something that Clough's near-contemporary Karl Marx might well have recognized – in 1845, Marx writes of 'the *something* [Etwas] of this clumsy world', a stubborn material core to reality that is bent on revolution.[21] Like Marx, what Clough sees within or beneath all the awfulness of history is 'something' that might just be ground for hope. Where Clough differs is that he entertains the possibility that what drives or informs history is not just some*thing* but some*one* – when Dipsychus meditates upon his destiny as a 'rebel' he suddenly breaks off to ask 'O, who sent me, though?' He then, enigmatically, answers himself: 'Some one, and to do something.'[22]

Conventionally, the 'someone' who sends the man of destiny into the world is that divine someone, God. Dipsychus, though, does not have God in mind. Neither does Clough; since Dipsychus's 'some*one*' leads to 'some*thing*', we are made to think of the man whom Claude saw killed – he too is some*one* who gives way to some*thing*: 'I have seen a man' soon becomes 'I saw something'. In Clough the someone driving history (the someone who 'sends' us into history) appears not to be God but rather someone who is killed, a man who is killed. In the poem 'Adam and Eve', Clough's Adam talks to Cain about the 'fatal fact' of death that is Cain's 'earliest revelation of the world'; at the very beginning of history is the fatal fact of fatality, a fact which Cain himself has confirmed by killing his brother Abel and thereby committing the world's first murder.[23] For Clough, the inaugural fact of history is the fatal fact that a man is killed. Witness Clough's intense interest in the man who is killed not only in Eden but Rome, this is not just the man Claude saw killed but also no less a world-historical figure than Julius Caesar: Clough's submission for the 1840 Newdigate Prize at Oxford is a poem called 'The Judgement of Brutus', that most famous of Caesar's assassins.[24]

The fatal fact of assassination is a familiar fact of history, but one that preys strangely upon Clough's mind. In April 1855 Clough writes an odd, musing letter to William Allingham from his London office in Downing Street:

> Here we sit at 5pm waiting to see from our Office windows the French Emperor and Empress pass on their way from Bricklayers Arms Station to the Great Western – They should have been here before this, but I suppose it is not on account of some refugee's pistol.[25]

Clough is right – it is not on account of a pistol; as Clough's letter goes on to explain, there was no attempt at assassination, the emperor and empress were simply late for their train. Here, for a moment, Clough entertains the possibility that a world-historical killing has just taken place; in the very next moment that possibility is gone, a world-historical figure has *not* been killed. This, however, is 1855, when London was buzzing with what Clough himself calls 'wars and rumours of wars'[26] – in particular, the Crimean War; one man has *not* been killed in London, but the fact remains that many are being killed in Scutari. The fatal fact of history is that a man is always being killed somewhere; if it is not the French emperor then it is a soldier.

Indeed, if it is not a soldier at war, then it might just be a worker under capitalism; this is the buried, ironic lesson of 'Mari Magno', where we are told the 'history' of the young French soldier who, having survived the battle for Rome, began a business trading with 'some mines of lead,/ Worked by an

English company'.[27] The soldier thus exchanges soldiering, or the business of killing, for a business which could itself kill – in nineteenth-century lead mines, death by explosion, suffocation and other forms of accident was far from uncommon. Just as hazardous were the 'slate quarries' of north Wales through which Clough records walking in a diary entry for 15 September 1842; these were quarries where the use of gunpowder had caused many violent deaths.[28] Clough makes no mention whatsoever of these deaths; as he writes in an earlier diary, 'we ... walk ... in a state of unconsciousness to most of the terrible realities existing about us'.[29]

Clough once wrote of 'the need to call to mind/ Our slaving brother', but Clough knows this to be profoundly difficult – if only because, as T. S. Eliot writes, 'human kind/ Cannot bear very much reality'.[30] Claude may well have seen a man killed but he grows uncertain simply because he cannot bear the thought. There is in Clough a sense that history cannot quite be thought, that it has a life beyond or outside our conscious day-time minds. According to Hegel, 'History [is] the great Day's work of Spirit', but Clough seems more persuaded by Carlyle who, writing in 1831, declares that 'now there is darkness, and long watching till it be morning'.[31] In Clough we are close to what the modernist writer Djuna Barnes would call 'history at night', a vision of history as a strange or terrible dream; writing to Blanche in 1851, Clough darkly announces,

> here in this ... night-time of existence we grope about ... run up against each other ... and do we know not what.[32]

To quote *The Bothie*, 'If there is battle, 'tis battle by night'; of Oxford's religious controversies Clough writes, 'like men in a night-battle we know not friend from foe'.[33] Exactly the same image recurs when, in 'Dover Beach', Matthew Arnold attempts to define the mid-century moment; this landmark poem ends with the 'confused alarms' of the 'ignorant armies [that] clash by night'.[34] Such alarms can certainly be heard or overheard in Clough as here and there he talks, variously, of 'a nightmarch', a 'night-missive', 'stray soldiers', 'a random shot' and a man that 'die[s] ... mistaken'.[35]

Of course, if a random shot were to hit a stray soldier then a man might well die mistaken; in which case Claude could be right, he could have seen a man killed. If so, both Claude and Clough could then be assured that history *can* happen 'here', before their very eyes. Clough can never quite believe this. For Clough, it is always just possible that the man was not killed, that history is not taking place – or at least not 'here', not with *him* around. This is the lesson of Clough's eccentric letter about the French emperor and the refugee's pistol; in this case there is not even 'a random shot'. Here history has, most conspicuously, *not* happened. But such is the nature of history at night – this is the history that does not quite happen, where paths do not quite cross and contacts are not quite made:

> Here in this ... night-time of existence we grope about and run up against each other, and peer blindly but enquiringly into strange faces ... [Though] sooner or later ... [we] clasp hands and make vows [we then] ... withdraw again and wrench away [our] hands.[36]

This is existence without point or conclusion, a history of disappointment. Equally anti-climactic is the night-time history glimpsed in the poem 'A woman fair and stately'; the woman, it turns out, is a strange kind of night-time historian whose ending is, well, not an ending:

> A woman fair and stately
>   Yet pale as are the dead
> Oft in the watches of the night
>   Sat spinning by his bed,
> And as she plied the distaff
>   In a sweet voice and low
> She sang of great old houses,
>   And fights fought long ago;
> So sat she, and so sang she
>   Until the east was grey,
> Then pointed to her bleeding breast
>   And shrieked and fled away.[37]

What makes this story of the night-time historian so anti-climactic is that it ends with a death (if it is a death) that comes as a surprise and is quite unlike the heroic battlefield deaths of 'fights fought long ago'. At night, it seems, there is bleeding but no sword, or bullet, to pierce the skin; there is sudden flight but no obvious cause for alarm. History at night is *un*history, an uncanny combination of strange event and non-event. This combination is, at once, both tragic and comic; the bleeding woman's shriek is pure mock-Gothic, we do not know whether to laugh or cry. Cue Karl Marx famously trying to remember what Hegel once said:

> Hegel remarks somewhere that all facts and personages of great importance in world history occur, so to speak, twice. He forgot to add: the first time as tragedy, the second time as farce.[38]

This axiom is, for Marx, most spectacularly evidenced in 1851 when, fifty-two years after Napoleon Bonaparte seized absolute power, exactly the same trick was performed by Napoleon's nephew, Louis Napoleon. This second Napoleonic coup, argues Marx, was no more than a self-conscious parody of the first; Louis Napoleon was simply a case of history happening for the second time. Clough goes further, identifying Louis Napoleon with history that does not even happen once: this 'wonderful melodramatic genius', as Clough wryly called him, is the same French emperor who, in April 1855, is *not* the target of 'a refugee's pistol'.[39] This is the second time that Louis Napoleon is around when history does not happen: in April 1848, when he is himself a refugee in London, Louis volunteers to be one of the many special constables enlisted by a government gripped by the misguided fear that the Chartists' demonstration on Kennington Common would lead to revolution. As it happened, the demonstration, much smaller than expected, was, in John Goode's words, 'a pathetic non-event'.[40] As Matthew Arnold reports to Clough on the day itself,

> The crowd disperse[d]. – Then came an hour after, the hard rain ... – There may be a little row in the evening ... but nothing much, I think.[41]

Revolution may be sweeping across continental Europe – 'these', writes Clough, 'were the days of ... Declarations ... Barricades ... Arms ... [and] Neufchatel rifles'; however, back in England, revolution is dissolving in the London rain.[42] Clough can write as much as he likes of a 'fanaticised Europe' and 'Paris millenniums' but, as Arnold languidly reminds him, 'the millennium won't come this bout', by which he seems also to mean 'won't come *here* about'.[43] In February 1848 Clough remarks to Arnold that 'the French have begun a new revolution

... [whilst] meantime, in England we go on in our usual humdrum way'.[44]

For Clough, there is something about mid-Victorian England that stops history happening; witness the satirical and prescient poem 'To the Great Metropolis', where Clough complains that busy, fashionable and congested London is not so much 'a mighty Nation's heart' as a massive 'railway terminus'.[45] Clough's modern England has at the very centre of its being a train station. As Dipsychus declares with spectacular bathos,

> ... The modern Hotspur
> Shrills not his trumpet of 'To Horse, To Horse!'
> But consults columns in a railway guide.[46]

So perverse is the railway age that even the proud and passionate Hotspur (the soldier-hero of Shakespeare's *1 Henry IV*) is reduced to studying train timetables – as well he might, the English railway boom of the 1840s producing, almost overnight, a whole new concern with uniform time. For Dipsychus, preoccupation with railway time serves only to diminish England's sense of historical time: modern Hotspurs may 'dream of arms and conflicts', but in reality they 'are set' to do no more than 'fold up papers'. Just a few years later, with the outbreak of the Crimean War in 1854, dreams of arms and conflicts did possess modern, railway England; but Clough himself really was set merely to fold up papers, the papers of Florence Nightingale. As the war progressed, Clough became an almost slavish amanuensis of the now-famous nurse; for Clough, no task was too menial – as official secretary to the 'Nightingale Fund' he quite literally folded papers. He also assisted by consulting the columns of railway guides as both nurses and supplies were dispatched to the Crimea by train.[47] In October 1854 Clough accompanied Nightingale herself as far as Calais, but he went no further; it was Nightingale, not Clough, who took the train to war, the train to history.[48]

TRAIN

> ... and is it not going to rain?
>
> *(Amours de Voyage)*[49]

When Clough finds himself in the middle of besieged Rome, it could be said that he has inadvertently caught the train to history; however, when Clough depicts his Rome experience in *Amours de Voyage* the great comic theme that surrounds the defiantly touristic Claude is his spectacular *in*capacity to engage with history. Claude's very first letter from the Eternal City opens with the frank admission that 'Rome disappoints me much'; this is followed, in the second letter, with: 'what do I want with this rubbish of ages departed ...?'[50] Even the onset of the siege leaves Clough himself rather unimpressed – 'it is funny', he writes to Tom Arnold, 'how much like any other city a besieged city looks'.[51] Might, then, Rome in some sense look like London? For Claude, perhaps it does; though he claims that 'Rome ... is other than London', he seems to encounter much the same weather.[52] Epitomizing the great English preoccupation with the elements, Claude's very first letter almost immediately announces that 'the weather is truly horrid'. Claude returns to this theme when, at the very height of the siege, he declares that 'we stand in the sun, but [are] afraid of a probable shower'.[53] When in Rome, Claude thinks not as the Romans do but as the English do; he takes the weather with him. The weather he takes ('the probable shower') is much the same as the weather that marked the end of the Chartist demonstration in London just one year before: 'then came an hour after, the hard rain'.

What makes the two weathers so similar is that, like Arnold's hard rain, Claude's probable shower encodes a self-consciously English dismissal, or rejection of history. In 1862 Victor Hugo remarked that 'if it had not rained on ... [the eve of Waterloo] the fate of Europe would have been changed'[54]; according to Hugo, rain can actually make history but, for Claude in Rome and Arnold in London, rain (or at least *talking* about the rain) unmakes history. In each case, talking about the weather is a way of avoiding or undermining any sense of historical moment. This happens again in *Dipsychus*, where the Spirit suddenly abandons his grand discourse on 'God, Revelation, and the rest of it' with a spectacularly banal reference to the weather: 'And now I think the rain has ended ... the less said, the sooner mended.'[55] Talk of rain is a way of avoiding the grand narrative of history ('God, Revelation, and the rest of it'); Cloughean rain encodes a need for a little, or private, narrative of history. Talk of a 'probable shower' is Claude's way of carving his own space out of the massive historical moment in which he is caught, a space that is forever England, forever Claude. It is also forever Clough – in his diaries he too uses rain to measure or mark out private time. When on solitary walking holidays, Clough often makes a reference to the day's rainfall; occasionally, 'Heavy Rain' is the entry for the day.[56] The rain does not, of course, fall only on Clough, but by becoming part of a diary entry it is, to some extent, privatized. In and through the English rain, public time and private time imperceptibly dissolve into each other.

In Rome things are different. Here private and public time throw each other into dramatic and even absurd relief; writing from the besieged city, Clough observes that 'the World perhaps in the same day will lose the Vatican and me!'[57] This theme finds splendid comic echo in *Amours de Voyage* when Claude relates how, with the French at the very gates of Rome, his first thought is of lunch: 'I go', he writes, 'to make sure of my dinner before the enemy enter.' As Claude later asks, 'What's the/ Roman Republic to me ...?'[58] The answer, he implies, is very little or nothing; but some of Clough's contemporaries believed very strongly that world-history and the individual life were intimately related. The key figure in this was the American transcendentalist Ralph Waldo Emerson whom Clough admired, and met in 1848; this was a year after the publication of 'History', an essay in which Emerson announces the existence of a profound sympathy or 'relation between the hours of our life and the centuries of time'; we are right, he declares, to

> sympathise in the great moments of history ... [for] in the great discoveries, the great resistances [and] the great prosperities of men ... [the] ... law was enacted ... the land was formed, or the blow was struck *for us*, as we ourselves in that place would have done.[59]

For this reason,

> all history becomes subjective ... [and] there is properly no history;
> only biography ... All public facts are to be individualised ... all
> private facts are to be generalised ... History becomes fluid, and true
> ... Biography deep and sublime.

This is, in many ways, an after-echo of Romanticism and its
profound interfusing of self and world, particular and individual – an interfusing that is most spectacularly glimpsed in a
famous letter written by the philosopher Hegel from within the
besieged Prussian city of Jena. On the very day in October 1806
that Jena fell to Napoleon's imperial army, Hegel writes,

> I saw the Emperor – that World Soul – riding out of the city on
> reconnaissance. It is indeed a wonderful sensation to see such an
> individual, who, concentrated here at a single point, astride a horse,
> reaches out over the world and masters it.[60]

For Hegel, at this single point, history really *is* biography; both
meet in 'that World Soul,' Napoleon Bonaparte. Indeed, history
and biography, the world and I, also meet in the simple yet
sublime phrase, 'I saw the Emperor', a phrase that is heightened
still further when Dipsychus, in a strangely visionary moment of
martial glory, declares: 'I see Napoleon on the heights, intent/ To
arrest that one brief unit of loose time/ Which hands high
Victory.'[61] Loose time could not be more dramatically arrested;
here world and I, Napoleon and I, meet in a moment of total, or
pure history. In Clough, such moments are always precarious.
Just as Claude's 'I saw a man killed' is immediately revised and
questioned, so Dipsychus's 'I saw Napoleon' is always already
undermined – if only because it is a phrase that, by the mid-
nineteenth century, has become a catch-phrase of the little
man's claim to world-historical significance. In 1852 Clough
writes a satirical letter about the old man he meets in America
who claims 'I saw Napoleon crowned Emperor'; he also, adds
Clough, claims that he 'saw the present Sultan ride through
Constantinople ... – *and so on*'.[62] We are some way from Hegel's
momentous 'I saw the Emperor'; and we are still further when,
in 1855, Clough himself gets to see Napoleon, since in Clough's
case it is that modern, sham-Napoleon, Louis Napoleon; he
who, far from leading imperial armies across Prussia, is hurrying
through London late for a train:

> Here we sit at 5pm waiting to see…the Emperor and Empress pass on their way … to the Great Western – They should have been here before this.

In the age of the train it is not just the modern Hotspur who needs a railway guide but also the modern Napoleon. This, presumably, is 'loose time' or what Hamlet famously calls 'time … out of joint'.[63] What is out of joint, or loose, is the connection between the little man and big history, or I and Napoleon. Whereas Napoleon and Hegel somehow share the same world-historical moment (namely, the capture of Jena) Napoleon and Clough have no such moment to share, despite Clough's attempt to think one into existence by imagining an assassination.

In doing so, Clough only loosens still further the connection between private and public; for, just days before, someone really did die – namely, Clough's first-born child: 'we have had the misfortune', he writes in a letter, 'to lose [our] … little boy, who was born suddenly to live only half a day'.[64] It is within days of the intensely private death of his own child that Clough is fancifully toying with the possibility of the very public death of an emperor. This public death does not take place; ironically, the real death (the real history) happens in the little and private world of Clough's family. Dipsychus talks of 'matters too, too small/ For any record on the leaves of time'; such a matter is the death of Clough's too, too small child – it is invisible to what Carlyle calls 'the eye of History'.[65] The irony of this particular unrecorded matter is that it is of more substance and weight than the recorded matter of the emperor's routine progress across London. Pertinent here is a strange line of Claude's that Clough, in the end, discarded; wandering amongst the giant historical architecture of Rome, Claude declares

> Great is Antiquity … but I, if I am small, *am* small.[66]

Claude seeks to remind us that what we might call 'the *I* of history' has being, or existence: I must not forget that 'I *am*'; indeed, Claude implies that, therefore, 'I' (however small) am necessarily greater than the greatest antiquity.

Arnold once addressed Clough as 'you poor subjective, you'.[67] Arnold was right, Clough does play the part of the poor subjective I of history – one thinks of Claude and his lunch. At such moments, Clough is very obviously at odds with the grand and objective I/eye of history, not only the I of the great soldier (Hegel's Napoleon) but also the eye of the great artist. When recalling Michelangelo's dome in the Sistine Chapel, Clough writes

> From far and near
> He drew the scattered ciphers
> Struck the decisive line, and with one look
> Sum totalled the experience of the world.[68]

In this particular poem Clough himself strikes no decisive line, in fact he only writes one more before abandoning the poem; as if overwhelmed by the very thought of a total account of the experience of the world, Clough cannot even manage a total poem. This is 'just' a fragment. If Clough does wish to 'solve the Universe' (as Arnold claimed) then here he fails quite spectacularly.[69] But that is because he lives in a culture which was uncomfortable with certain early-nineteenth-century attempts to think, or dream, in total, universal terms – whether that be Romanticism's poetic dream of 'World Soul' or Hegel's philosophical dream of 'Absolute Knowledge'. These visions from the early years of the century do not simply vanish; they are, in many ways, continued by such as Emerson. However, any grand, or total vision is bound to struggle in the pragmatic Age of Steam, or what Carlyle called 'the Age of Machinery'; writing in 1833, Edward Bulwer-Lytton observes, 'when Byron passed away [in 1824] ... we turned to the actual and practical ... we awoke from ... the passionate [and] the dreaming'.[70] Dreaming of a World Soul, or Spirit was now particularly difficult given that the Age of Machinery brought to the fore a middle class whose literary culture had, as its focal point, not the sublime landscapes of Romanticism or the historical vistas of Hegelianism, but rather the privatized space of the bourgeois home, or hearth. Along with this very enclosed place came its psychic mirror-image – the enclosed, or isolated mind. As Arnold writes in 1853, 'objectivity [has] ... disappeared; the dialogue of the mind with itself has commenced.'[71]

WAIT

>   ... but he, he waits.
>
>   (*Dipsychus*)[72]

For many of Arnold's generation the disappearance of objectivity, or the movement inward, necessarily meant a kind of solitary confinement. This, though, is not true of 'poor subjective' Clough who never forgets that the self only ever exists in time and, in particular, the present – a present that Clough sees as a strangely *open* space. As Emerson writes, 'the present is infinite', a claim given almost scientific force by Carlyle who writes that 'time, like space, is infinitely divisible'.[73] Carlyle's explosive insight parallels a number of contemporaneous scientific developments which, in various ways, were dividing time into smaller and smaller units – a process that culminated, in 1876, with Eadweard Muybridge's famous high-speed photography of a galloping horse. The series of photographs, each showing the horse in fractionally different positions, succeeded, as Rebecca Solnit puts it, in *'splitting the second*, as dramatic an action as splitting the atom'.[74] Clough did not live to see these photographs, but his writing does suggest an awareness of the physics and mathematics that made them possible. Clough talks of the 'infinitesimal moment', whilst Dipsychus, who '[has] hardly ... the courage to die outright', would 'somehow halve ... it' – he seeks to halve the moment of death.[75] Just a few lines later, as death draws ever closer, Dipsychus is desperately seeking to divide up time still further:

> Is the hour here, then? Is the minute come –
> The irreprievable instant ...
> ...
> O for a few, few grains in the running glass.

Claude asks, 'Did we really believe that the Present ... is the Only!' – clearly Dipsychus wishes it were; but the running glass (like Muybridge's running horse) tells us otherwise, tells us that the present is insubstantial and elusive.[76]

Dipsychus underlines this troubling message by reminding us that the present occupies the almost unthinkably small space that exists between past and future, what Dipsychus calls 'this narrow interspace, this moment'.[77] For Clough's generation this interspace is first mapped by Carlyle who, in 1830, declares that man 'lives between two eternities ... Future and ... Past'.[78] A generation later, Carlyle's definition of what it means to inhabit the present becomes a definition of what it means to inhabit the mid-nineteenth century: we are 'wandering', writes Arnold, 'between two worlds, one dead/ The other powerless to be born'.[79] Clough is in a similar no-man's-land when he declares that the increasingly anomalous business of being an Oxford don is 'a mere parenthetical occupation, uncontemplated in the past and wholly alien to the future'.[80] For Clough, the narrow interspace that is the present (or at least the present as experienced by an Oxford don) is extremely narrow, extremely close. It is not, necessarily, too close for comfort – in July 1848 (still several months before resigning) Clough confesses that 'my existence is one *jubilant* alone'. This aloneness or narrowness is, though, *for Emerson*, too close for sanity;[81] insisting as he does on an intimate 'relation between the hours of our life and the centuries of time', Emerson goes on to suggest, very acutely, that attention to history 'remedies the defect of our too great nearness to ourselves'.[82] According to Emerson, history gets us away from ourselves, exposing us to distances of time that are far greater than an individual life. At Oxford, Clough is just beginning to sense these great distances; indeed, if Clough really does experience Oxford life as a mere parenthesis, trapped between past and future, he comes very close to Carlyle's living 'between two eternities'.

Clough feels the pressure of these eternities still more acutely after leaving Oxford. In one particular post-Oxford poem, Clough declares,

> On either side the demons wait
> To seize, distort, and mutilate.[83]

Outside Christian Oxford, Clough is exposed to forces or eternities that are anything but Christian; it is as if Clough recalls a particular letter from his friend J. C. Shairp – writing in September 1848, Shairp warns that leaving Oxford would mean Clough being

> cut off from the future of Christianity ... [and indeed] commit[ting] himself to the opposite side.[84]

These are peculiarly strong words; to leave Oxford, warns Shairp, is not only to leave the safety of orthodox, Christian history but also to join 'the opposite side' – a dark side. The demons wait not only 'on either side' but also *out*side, outside of the official, sanctioned time of Christian Oxford .

When time is loose, or out of joint, the wary Clough is on the lookout both for strange things and for strange figures; in 'The Judgement of Brutus' the 'strange time' of night is swiftly followed by talk of 'some strange guest that must not enter in'.[85] This alien or stranger may frighten, but whether s/he is demon or angel, friend or foe, is not clear; to quote the Spirit in *Dipsychus*: 'how the devil can you know/ Whether I am a devil or no?' – 'for aught your silly conscience knows', he might just be 'the Angel Gabriel in plain clothes'.[86] He might even be a demon in Christ's clothes: when Clough writes of the demons that wait to mutilate, he immediately goes on to write, no less enigmatically, that

> More than ten thousand miles away
> A child is born – a joyful sound;
> Wrap him in swaddling clothes around
> And in his cradle lay him fair.[87]

One moment it is demons, the next it is a faraway Christ, or at least a child dressed, like Christ, in swaddling clothes. Clough's strange guest (the guest that haunts 'strange time') is again a kind of Christ when, just two or three months before the infamous resignation, Clough's Oxford diaries come to a bizarre climax of almost Messianic anticipation; addressing himself, Clough cries,

> Not in vain, O Poor Poetaster, not in vain though life's total be summed up in one seeming-vain expectancy! ... Not in vain, though ... thou thyself to thy own self-contempt ... seemest ... some portentously deluded Joanna Southcote, lying in of a Messiah that is flatulence ...[88]

Joanna Southcote was a psychic maid who believed she had supernatural powers and who, in October 1813, declared she was pregnant with a spiritual being called Shiloh. Charged with anticipation of life-after-Oxford, Clough invokes the eager expectancy of a would-be Virgin Mary; at this the strangest

49

time in his life, Clough imagines himself as one awaiting that strangest of guests, the Messiah.

In doing so, Clough joins with those for whom every moment is charged with Messianic anticipation: the Jews. As Walter Benjamin would remark, 'for the Jews ... every second of time [is] ... the straight gate through which the Messiah might enter'.[89] In an early draft of *Amours de Voyage*, Mary Trevellyn confesses, 'I somehow have faith in waiting'; it is a seemingly casual line, but one that again invokes the figure of the Jew – he who waits *in* faith, or as an *act* of faith.[90] Strange though it may seem, there is (here and there) a Jewish Clough. In another early draft, this time for 'Mari Magno', the restless Clough has one character declare that the restless and itinerant English are 'descended of the Wandering Jew'.[91] One biblical Jew who famously wandered was Jacob – he who, having 'wrestled with the Lord', limped for ever after, thus giving rise to the popular nineteenth-century legend that the Jew is lame. Each of Clough's major poems has, at its centre, a character identified as lame: in *The Bothie* Philip Hewison claims that he is 'lame' (well might Hobbes ask, 'and is not Philip a Jacob?'); whilst, in *Amours de Voyage*, there is Claude, whose name comes from the Latin for 'limping' – namely, *claudus*.[92] This would not have been lost on Clough's erudite readership; and they would also know that Clough refers to the seventeenth-century Dutch-Jewish philosopher Baruch Spinoza when, in 1849, Clough concludes one particular poem with the lines:

> That moment
> ... in Amsterdam
> Sat one who knew and said
> The finite is the infinite, Man, God.[93]

'That moment' is the uncanny instant in which 'a man', having dreamt or imagined that he is travelling or progressing, wakes to 'find ... himself wherever he had started from'. Spinoza, though, sits and knows that to end where you started is only right and proper, since the 'infinite', being somehow also 'finite', is *here and now*; and likewise, since 'God' is somehow also 'Man' then he too is *here and now*. Spinoza is not only one who sits and knows but also one who sits and waits, though he does not expect to wait long (or indeed any time at all); unlike Walter

Benjamin's Jew, the pantheistic Spinoza believes that every second of time is the straight gate through which the Messiah *does* enter – or has, in fact, always already entered.

Clough does not share Spinoza's confidence; he fears that any Messiah he might believe in is merely hot air, that (like Joanna Southcote) he is waiting for 'a Messiah that is flatulence' – no more than a fart. Clough fears that he waits for a Messiah that does not materialize, does not arrive. This is, most obviously, the Christ who does not come back from the dead; Clough's 'sad Gospel' is that 'Christ is not risen'. The fear of waiting in vain is, though, a more generalized Cloughean fear, a fear that repeats upon both his life and writing. The lovelorn Claude is 'waiting for nothing'; ironically, Mary, the woman for whom he waits, feels much the same: 'Well, [Claude] … is not come; and now, I suppose, he will not come'.[94] Again, the Oxonian Clough talks of 'waiting, upon the Isis … [for]/ The boats that should have passed there and did not'. As Clough writes elsewhere, 'the hour may come, and come in vain'.[95] On 19 June 1850 the hour in question is, to be precise, seven o'clock in the morning; in a peculiar postscript to a letter written to Shairp, Clough remarks,

> All these things I have been writing while waiting for a pupil, between 7 and 8am, who does not come.[96]

Waiting, it seems, is simply what Clough does; like Cain (to quote Clough's shortest-ever sentence), 'He waits.' In 'Mari Magno', the tale significantly called 'My Tale' begins: 'I waited.' Since, though, the hour may 'come in vain', the question is (to quote an earlier tale): '*Why* do I wait?'[97] If we return to that postscript of 19 June 1850, Clough's perverse answer is that he waits because that is when he writes; if he were not having to wait for his pupil he would not have written the letter to Shairp: 'all these things I have been writing while waiting'. What we do while waiting for someone who does not turn up is an important question for Clough; whilst waiting for Claude who 'is not come', Mary asks Miss Roper, 'What will you think, meantime?'[98] If Clough *writes* whilst waiting for someone who does not come, and Miss Roper *thinks* whilst waiting for someone who does not come, then Mary *asks* about thinking whilst waiting for someone who does not come. Writing, thinking, asking – all, it seems, are things done whilst waiting; it is as if all life were a form of waiting. If we are like the Lawyer in 'Mari Magno' who is 'wait[ing] to die', then life is merely what happens whilst we are waiting.[99] This is the overwhelming lesson of that classic of twentieth-century boredom, Samuel Beckett's *Waiting for Godot* (1953), the play about two tramps for whom life consists in nothing more or less than finding ways to pass the time whilst waiting for someone called Godot who does not turn up. Clough is waiting for Godot a hundred years too early.

To put this another way, Clough anticipates the twentieth-century conviction that if God is dead then history is emptied of meaning; to quote Dipsychus's atheistic Spirit, 'Methinks I see ... void time'.[100] The Spirit is unusual in this; very few mid-Victorians saw time as void. It is true that the scientific developments which often prompted unbelief in the 1830s and 1840s revealed a world that was much older than anyone had hitherto believed and thus opened up vast new vistas of time; however, this was not quite 'void time' since even those geologists who were beginning to question the existence of God still envisaged a world charged with purpose and progress – theories of evolution were circulating well before Darwin's *On the Origin of Species* (1859). So too were theories of devolution, or dissolution, particularly among solar physicists such as William Thomson, who argued that the sun (and, therefore, the universe) was slowly cooling; in 1852 Thomson declared that 'there is ... in the material world a universal tendency to the dissipation of mechanical energy'.[101] If, as Isaac Newton had insisted, the universe was a vast clockwork machine, then for Thomson the clock was running down. And that is precisely the image invoked by Claude when, having waited in vain for Mary, he declares he is 'like a running-down watch'.[102] Here Clough's degenerative vision of time does coincide with contemporary science; what makes Clough different is that his vision is so vividly marked by theology – when Claude sees void time, he sees 'everlasting *limbos* of void time'. The word 'limbo' is a term from medieval theology denoting the abode of souls excluded from heaven but not condemned to hell, in particular the righteous souls who lived before Christ, and who would remain in limbo until Christ's Second Coming. The void, or nothing, that the Spirit sees is, then, a special kind of nothing, a nothing marked by the activity of waiting, by sacred waiting. There may be no point in waiting – these are, after all, 'everlasting limbos' – but despite that, or rather because of that, the act of waiting becomes a sacred act. Like Mary Trevellyn, Clough may 'somehow have *faith* in waiting'.

Those who wait in Clough certainly keep holy company; though most may only be waiting for a train, a boat, or a letter, they wait alongside those who are *waiting for God*. This is a phrase with two senses – you can wait for God to come or you can wait on God's behalf, because God asked you to do so. Thus, in Clough, we have not only those who wait for the resurrected Christ but also, and more curiously, a host of angels who, for one reason or another, have been commissioned to wait. In 'Repose in Egypt,' 'visible [are] angels waiting on' the exiled Christ-child; in 'Jacob' 'angels at nightfall [are] waiting at their door'.[103] These waiting angels are by no means simply good; Jacob's door-keeping angels are, in fact, positively hybrid, a cross between two very different sets of biblical angels. On the one hand, they are suggestive of the angels who, in Genesis chapter 18, appear to Jacob's grandfather Abraham as 'he sat in the tent door':

> Not ...
> As Isaac's days or Abraham's, have been mine;
> Not as the days of those that in the field
> Walked at eventide to meditate,
> And haply to the tent returning found
> Angels at nightfall waiting at their door.

On the other hand, these same angels are suggestive of the angels who, in Genesis chapter 19, are surrounded 'at even' by the men of Sodom, all wild with desire for them – the angels only escape by withdrawing into a house and 'shut[ting] ... the door'.[104] Jacob's waiting angels are as double as Dipsychus, they are at once both the angels who announce to Abraham that his aged wife is miraculously with child and yet also the angels who are all but raped on the street in Sodom. Whilst Abraham's angels merely bring news of conception, merely report on the fleshy world of sexual history, the angels in Sodom come perilously close to taking part in that same history. But then, to be a waiting angel is, by definition, to succumb to time; to deal not just with heaven but also with earth. Dipsychus's Spirit talks playfully of an 'Angel ... in plain clothes', but all Clough's waiting angels necessarily wear plain clothes, the plain clothes of history.[105] Such angels communicate something of not only the strange holiness of waiting but also the risk involved in any truly Christian, or incarnational holiness – the risk of being-in-time. We return to that astonishing poem 'The Angel' with its command:

> Exist – come forth –
>
> …
>
> Go and perform [God's] mission there below
> Go – and as some ill-omened bird of night
> Half-bird, half-beast, with foul and dismal way
> Hover and flit about this human soul
>
> …
>
> *While the time, his time and thine – Exist.*[106]

It is hard to imagine a more direct juxtaposition of angel and time; the two are vitually thrown together, almost as they are in 1939 when, on the eve of World War II, Walter Benjamin famously dreamt of what he called 'the angel of history'.[107] We tend not to associate angels with anything as coarse as history but both Benjamin and Clough believe we *must* do so. There is enough in common between a Jewish Marxist on the run from Nazi Germany and a Victorian agnostic exiled from Christian Oxford for both to insist that if we are really to think about history we must first think of that strange and difficult thing: an angel who 'Exists' in time, in history. This, for Clough, means the narrow and perilous interspace between heaven and earth, spirit and flesh, miracle and rape, hope and despair. It also, not surprisingly, means the experience of exile – the 'visible angels' that attend Christ do so even when he is 'in Egypt' having fled from the child-killing Herod. Angels are again made visible in exile when, in a moving poem called 'Last Words', Clough imagines himself addressing a dying Napoleon, defeated and banished to St Helena:

> Doubtless – angels, hovering o'er thee
> In thine exile's sad abode,
> Marshalled even now before thee,
> Move upon that chosen road! [108]

Cloughean angels do not fear to tread the hardest roads of history; even when Napoleonic history narrows to the one-way street that is defeat, exile and death, there the angels go. If history means angels (angels that accompany us) then the cryptic message of this poem is that, even at its most narrow, history is a street that we do not walk alone, in single file. The lesson of 'Last Words' is that Emerson was wrong, history is not biography, not even Napoleon's biography; the historical figure, however great, exists only in relation to others, a host of others – Napoleon is surrounded by angels that are not only 'hovering o'er' him but also 'marshalled ... before' him. Though the angels move on ahead they are so focused upon Napoleon it is as if they are constantly looking back at him. Cloughean history is so crowded with angels that to exist in time is to be faced (whether we know it or not) by an angel. Clough tells the angel not only to 'Exist...[in] time, his time and thine' but also to 'Go ... flit about this human soul/ Flapping thy black temptation in his face'. In Clough, angels press their faces right into history: 'Angel faces came', we read, '[and] kept/ Their watch upon the land.'[109]

LOOK

> ... one future glance.
>
> (*Dipsychus*)[110]

In the poem 'Blank Misgivings', Clough cries, 'Look me in the face.' This cry, first set down around 1840, is specifically addressed to 'Mother Night'; by 1852 the night has grown so alien, so anonymous, that Clough will be content with any face, however strange: 'here', he writes, 'in this night-time of existence we grope about ... and peer blindly but enquiringly into *strange* faces'. For Clough, the dominant desire of existence, of being-in-time, is the desire to look into the face of one who is looking back at me. To quote another poem,

> My beloved, is it nothing
> When I see thee and thou me,
> *When we see each other see.*
> Is it nothing, my beloved?[111]

This is a poem about 'the inevitable motion [that]/ Bears me forth upon the line'; the motion is history and the line is time. 'I' am doomed to a solitary and linear existence; others may be travelling along parallel lines but we will never quite meet unless and until we turn to 'see each other see' and, indeed, see each other *see each other*. For Emerson, 'history is subjective', but Clough dreams of a history that is (somehow) *inter*-subjective, a form of face-to-face encounter. Crucial to this is St Paul's famous declaration that though 'now we see [Christ] through a glass, darkly' at the last we shall see him *'face to face'*.[112] And it is this vision that Clough draws upon when he writes of that eventual moment 'when face to face we see/ The Father of our souls'.[113]

Such apocalyptic vision is not, though, sufficient for Clough; he wants to know not what we *will* be, but 'what we are here!', here and now, *in* time, not *beyond* time. Clough's own answer is that here and now we are faced not by a divine face but another very human face. That is certainly how Hegel sees things in *The Phenomenology of Spirit* (1807), where he famously argues that 'I' am always already faced by another. If this were not the case 'I' would not know that 'I' exist; as Hegel himself puts it,

> Self-consciousness exists in and for itself when, and by the fact that, it so exists for another; that is, it exists only in being acknowledged .... Self-consciousness is [therefore] faced by another self-consciousness.[114]

Clough would have known, or at least known *of*, this celebrated parable of self and other, a parable that Clough effectively turns into a historical situation. What Hegel conceives philosophically, Clough imagines historically. Here again Napoleon is important; though both Hegel and Clough know what it means to say 'I saw Napoleon', it is only Clough who, staying with the parable, allows for the possibility that Napoleon might return my gaze, that Napoleon might see *me*. In the poem 'Last Words', Clough not only *addresses* Napoleon but asks 'Is it *this* .../ That ... / Thine ... eye beholds?'; since we do not know what 'this' is (these are the very first words of the poem) we read with the possibility that it is Clough whom Napoleon's eye beholds. If Napoleon can hear Clough then perhaps Napoleon can see him. We should not forget that Clough met no less a historical figure than Giuseppe Mazzini, leader of the new Italian Republic: Clough had a half-hour private meeting with Mazzini just days before the siege of Rome in April 1849. For these thirty minutes Clough catches the eye of history, the eye of Rome.

Just a couple of months later Clough twice writes, 'it is funny to see how much like any other city a besieged city looks'.[115] To misread this as being about how the besieged city *looks* – looks *at Clough* – may itself seem 'funny', but it is only to recall Clough's early poem on the Indian city of Salsette, where he 'gaze[s] in wonder on the gazing wall'.[116] When Clough, a few years later, writes about 'the spying, prying, prating/ Of a curious cruel world', the 'of' is ambiguous, and so too the word 'curious': the cruel world might itself be spying and prying on *us*, might just be curious *about us*.[117] This proves true of the cruel world of history; trapped in besieged Rome, Claude announces, 'It is a curious history, this.'[118] It is never more curious than when Claude declares that 'I have seen a man killed'; in this case the really curious curiosity might be the curiosity of the man who has been killed. Claude's declaration begs the haunting question: did the man whom Claude has just seen being killed *see* Claude seeing him being killed? Did he catch Claude's eye? Did they 'see each other see'? We shall never know. Claude does not attempt to enter the mind of the man whom he saw being killed. That task is left to writers who belong to the still more terrible times of the twentieth century, most famously Franz Kafka, who ends his novel *The Trial* (1925) with the killing of the central character, simply called 'K.'; in the very moment of being killed, K. looks up to see what he thinks is someone at a window looking on:

> Who was it? Someone who sympathized? Someone who wanted to know?[119]

That someone is Claude. K. returns Claude's gaze from the future, the future of killing.

This is a conceit, or figure of speech, but in 'Adam and Eve' Clough does stare resolutely into the terrible face of future human suffering; having just eaten of the forbidden fruit, Eve cries:

> ... Ah me! alas! alas!
> More dismally in my face stares the doubt,
> More heavily on my heart weighs the world.
> ...
> ... all [the] despondencies ... [and] despairs,
> Of multitudinous souls on souls to come
> In me imprisoned fight, complain, and cry.[120]

As Eve stares into the future of despair (seeing not just one man killed but a multitude) these victims-to-be appear to 'complain and cry' out. They are not simply seen but actually return her gaze – to (mis)quote Eve: 'in my face stares ... the world'. The opportunity to stare back is not shared by the man whom Claude sees killed; Claude is too busy questioning the 'experience'. The poem reflects the letter in which Clough himself relates an actual killing: having told his friend Francis Palgrave of 'an Italian priest who', soon after the fall of Rome, 'was undoubtedly killed' for 'talk[ing] ... publicly ... with a Frenchman', Clough suddenly changes the subject with the words: 'to return to my own experience'.[121] Clough anticipates what he was to write in quite another connection: namely, 'from history I am seducing you to self-observation'.[122] This comes from a lecture Clough gave at University College London in 1851, by which point Clough has himself been seduced away from history, or at least from the extreme history of besieged Rome and revolutionary Paris; within a year Clough would abandon Europe altogether to seek a career in America, that land which Hegel called the 'land of desire for all those who are weary of the historical lumber-room of old Europe'.[123] Not for the first time, America is seen to provide the passport to get out of history. In July 1849, this is quite literally the case for the leaders of the defeated Italian Republic; with Rome now fallen, the only way for Mazzini *et al.* to avoid arrest was to claim 'American protection'. As Clough observes, 'Mazzini ... got off with an American passport.'[124] Clough does too; when he travels to America in 1852, he is returning to where he lived as a child.

'Yankee Clough', as he was called at Rugby, was once declared (by Emerson) to be 'the best American', a remark strangely echoed when an English friend, trying to persuade him to stay in England, announced: 'we may [yet] have revolutions... – and you may be President!'[125] This vision of Clough as president of a republican England (as not only the best American but also the best Englishman) is all the more bizarre given that the president, or rather head of that most famous of republics – namely, France – had twice turned into an emperor. To imagine that 'Citizen Clough' might yet be 'President Clough' is, therefore, also to make thinkable Emperor Clough, a Clough who could say not only 'I see Napoleon' but also 'I *am* Napoleon'. Clough knows well the seductive attraction of such madness, the madness that Keats had called the 'egotistical sublime'.[126] This madness is there at the very beginning of Cloughean history: having eaten of the forbidden fruit Adam cries, 'I – seem eternal, O thou God, as Thou.'[127] It is also there at the modern end of Cloughean history: in besieged Rome, Claude confesses to dreaming of 'great indignations and angers transcendental... of a sword at my side and a battle-horse underneath me'.[128] Claude really has been seduced *from* history *to* self-observation; to be precise, this is the self-observation of that absolute Self, Napoleon, the soldier-Emperor. Twenty years after Napoleon's death Clough locates, within the petit-bourgeois Claude, the continuing dream of an absolute Self, or Subject; a dream, or nightmare, by which history becomes not just subjective but Subjective, the biography of the one strong man.

We might think that the nineteenth century, the century which ushers in so much democracy, would kill off the one strong man, but Clough knew better. For all his socialist instincts and support of Chartism, Clough has his doubts about democracy, what he calls 'the perilous gift of self-government'.[129] Clough once wrote that '*Vox Populi* [the voice of the people] is ... the din from the thousand voices of chaos and outer darkness'. At such moments Clough sounds alarmingly like Carlyle; the difference is that Carlyle, the author of *On Heroes, Hero-Worship and the Heroic in History*, despised democracy precisely because it would *not* cultivate the one strong and heroic man. Clough's counter-fear that democracy is, somehow, in love with tyranny has been proven right by the democratically elected monsters of the twentieth century. Indeed, in this connection, Clough looks forward still further, to the twenty-first century, and the world domination of that most self-conscious of democracies, America; when Clough reached America in 1852, he was confronted by the paradox of a democracy that was already busy creating, in the presidency, what would become the most powerful office in the history of the world. Clough comes very close to seeing this, particularly in his violent criticism of America's policy of aggression toward both Mexico and Cuba, a policy echoed in the chilling slogan 'Manifest Destiny'.[130] Clough parodies the policy as cannibalism, declaring that the American shall eat his fellow men through the whole world.

In *Amours de Voyage* Claude announces, 'I can be and become anything that I … look at'; what Clough sees in America is a democracy that believes much the same, that is threatening to turn Claude's egotistical sublime into a political reality, the reality of American imperialism.[131] Clough sees (or foresees) in America a democracy that declares, 'I can *eat* anything I look at.'

This dark line of thought implies criticism of the very act of looking; it reminds us that looks can kill. So too does the poem 'I said so, but it is not true' (1851), a quasi-Wordsworthian meditation upon sight and the ways in which it reduces the world to mere forgettable surface: 'we behold it, and it dies'.[132] As the poem proceeds, Clough talks, arrestingly, of 'the mere simplicity of what/ We saw – and looked on, and forgot'. 'We saw … and forgot' – with these words a meditation turns suddenly into something alarmingly close to confession, especially if read alongside Claude's 'I have seen a man killed'; for is this a case of '*I* looked on, and forgot'? In particular, forgot to act or intervene? The question of intervention troubles Claude, most obviously when he pleads:

> …What can I do? I cannot
> Fight, you know …
> …
> … In the first place, I haven't so much as a musket.
> In the next, if I had, I shouldn't know how I should use it.
> In the third, just at present I'm studying ancient marbles.
> In the fourth, I consider I owe my life to my country.
> In the fifth, – I forget, but four good reasons are ample.[133]

Claude looks and forgets, forgets why he cannot intervene. This is wit that anticipates Oscar Wilde, but it pales as soon as Claude adds, 'let 'em fight, and be killed'. This chilling disclaimer finds still more terrible echo in a line that Clough chose not to include – namely, Claude's astonishing endorsement of ancient Egypt's indifference as to the number of men killed in the building of a pyramid: 'let them/ Die,' he says, 'by the million or billion in misery'.[134] What is most shocking about this line is the sheer numbers; whilst the French and Italian soldiers whom Claude lets fight and be killed amounted 'only' to hundreds, here Claude appears willing to let millions and even billions be killed.

Claude goes way beyond the numbers ever killed in making pyramids; suddenly, he seems no longer to be thinking of ancient Egypt at all, but rather to have somehow wandered back into the killing fields of the nineteenth century. In the mid-forties a million had died in the Irish Famine, and did so in the age of steam-printing, telegraphy and rapid reportage; as Clough argued at the time, the English who watched them die in their newspapers were, necessarily, far from innocent.[135] This was a case of letting a million die in misery. However, to let millions die is a trick beyond the Victorians; only we who, in the age of television, can look on and forget those who are starving to death in Africa could even begin to let people die in such numbers. Claude's indifference to the deaths of others thus chances upon a terrible future. It is a future that is, in part, still ahead of us; for to talk of dying by the 'billion' puts us in mind of the atomic bomb. This, too, Clough chances upon when Adam, talking about the seed or 'atom' of a certain thought, declares that

> ... this rich atom some day,
> In some futurity of distant years – ...
> ...
> In some matured and procreant human brain may
> Germinate, burst, and rise into a tree.[136]

For us, who read this after Hiroshima, the thought of the atom so matures in the brain as to burst and rise into the image not of a tree but a mushroom, the mushroom-cloud of an atomic explosion.

Elsewhere, Clough talks of the future as the 'harvest which is not yet', but if Adam's atomic vision of that harvest is in any sense mushroom-shaped then the 'harvest which is not yet' is a terrible one.[137] No wonder Claude talks of 'trembling for the harvest'. He also declares,

> of this new epoch ... let us not dream of ... giving any representation.[138]

Clough does not want the future made visible; he suspects too much the whole business of looking and, in particular, the business of looking at the dead. In almost the same curious breath, Clough adds that he will lead us away from such sights:

> I am leading you unawares from a gallery of portraits of the dead through a door that opens upon a meeting of living, moving and acting men.

These are strange and spectacular words; particularly given that Clough is, in fact, giving a lecture on 'The Development of English Literature'. In doing so, he talks about much more – namely, a profoundly haunted future in which 'the dead' become 'living' as soon as they are no longer being looked at, no longer treated as 'a gallery of portraits'. This is a future that is also a strange kind of resurrection, a resurrection that comes from *not looking*. After all, if 'behold it and it *dies*' then, presumably: behold it *not* and it *lives*. For Claude, such 'logic' would mean that the man whom he saw killed would return to life as soon as he, Claude, is no longer looking at him. This, in turn, would mean that Claude could not control or even know what that man is doing, this man who is now 'living, moving and acting'. Indeed, if he is now 'meeting' with all the other once-dead men (of whom, as Claude reminds us, there are or will be millions and even billions) we are left with the possibility that the man Claude saw killed could yet coordinate a terrible collective revenge on all who have ever 'looked on, and forgot' – looked on and forgot the dead and the dying. The living, it seems, should be afraid of the dead. For Clough, the greatest shock of history is the shock of guilt.

> Well I remember ...
> How ...
> ... sudden at once
> Up from my side you started, screaming 'Guilt!'[139]

('Adam and Eve')

3

Hang Thinking:
The Thought of Death

> ... But that one
> ...
> ... whose sole office was to exist –
> Should suddenly dissolve and cease to be
> Calls up the hardest questions.
>
> ('Sonnets on the Thought of Death')[1]

THROUGH

After death we face questions, especially when no one has ever died before. When the world began, as Clough reminds us, 'we were meant to live for ever'; it was only with the Fall, with the eating of the forbidden fruit, that we learnt to die.[2] Well might Clough's Adam ask, 'what is ... death?' The same question is begged as Cain, having committed the world's first murder, struggles to make sense of the motionless body that lies before him:

> What? fallen? so quickly down, so easily felled,
> And so completely? Why, he does not move.
> Will he not stir – will he not breathe again?
> ...
> *Dead is it then?*[3]

This first ever death calls up particularly hard questions, and the hardest, or harshest, is: 'Dead is it then?' What makes this question so harsh, so unnerving, is that it calls up reason, or deduction: this body does not move, does not stir, does not breathe ... '*Dead* is it then?' Dead is it, *therefore*? Faced by the world's very first corpse, Cain neither weeps nor laughs, instead

63

he simply reasons, he draws on the resources of logic. Isobel Armstrong suggests that, in Clough, 'reasoning is not only a procedure but a theme' – a theme of death, it seems.[4] To quote Clough's Adam, 'eat we did, and *so* were doomed to die'; or, in the words of Dipsychus's Spirit, '*therefore* you ... die'.[5] The words 'therefore' and 'die' make for a terrible combination; there is something about bringing reason to bear on death that disturbs and disquiets: 'Dead is it *then?*'; '*so* ... we die'; '*therefore* you ... die' – each time Clough insists on reasoning death, or at least that we should know what it feels like when death is reasoned or, still worse, made reasonable. Clough, the poet whose theme is reason, does not stop reasoning in the face of death.

In Clough, mind or consciousness keeps going right up to the very instant of death, even the instant of my own death. Woody Allen once remarked that 'I'm not afraid to die, I just don't want to be there when it happens'; for Clough, I *am* there when it happens – the thinking, conscious 'I' *is* there. 'I lie', writes Clough, 'in my little coffin ... thinking.'[6] To quote Claude, 'I *know* that I bleed', 'I *know* ... I die'.[7] Clough keeps returning to he 'who upon death's immediate brink [is]/ Knowing'.[8] In this, Clough reflects his age, an age that did not have the drugs to ensure that I am *not* there when death happens. For many early Victorians it was very important that the dying person is present, is conscious right to the last; still hugely influential was the ancient Christian idea, or ideal of *ars moriendi* ('the art of dying'). This is the art of the good, or holy death, an art in which the dying person 'dies ... in full possession of his faculties, and professing the most perfect confidence of his acceptance with God' – so writes Richard Whateley in 1829.[9] Even with Christian belief beginning to decline, the Victorian cult or culture of death retained this emphasis on the knowing death. When A. P. Stanley writes to Clough about the death of Thomas Arnold, he makes a point of remarking: 'My belief is, though he never said it, that he knew that he was dying.'[10]

Clough certainly knew he was dying; that is why in July 1861, after a complete nervous and mental breakdown, he took doctor's advice and travelled across Europe searching in vain for the rest and climate that might save or extend his life.[11] Clough's fate is rehearsed in *Amours de Voyage*, where Claude, too, seems to know he is dying, or at least to be imagining what it is like to know one is dying. This is when he compares falling in love to lowering himself into a labyrinth secured by only a rope; so elaborate, though, is the conceit that its account of the perils of desire becomes a scrambled account of the perils of hanging:

> Lo, with the rope on my loins I descend through the fissure ...
> ...
> Still, wheresover I swing, wherever to shore, or to shelf
> ... I know I
> Yet shall one time feel the strong cord tighten about me, –
> ... and though the
> Rope sway wildly, I faint, crags wound me, from crag unto crag re-
> Bounding, or, wide in the void, I die ten deaths, ere the end I
> Yet shall plant firm foot on the broad lofty spaces I quit ...[12]

To précis: 'I swing ... I ... feel the ... cord tighten ... [and] the Rope sway ... I faint ... I die'; it is as if we are privy to the thoughts of one who is being hanged. Clough once remarked, 'give a dog a bad name and hang him, give a *boy* a bad name and he will hang himself', and Clough is himself just such a boy as soon as he walks out of Oxford.[13] Clough's bad name is 'Judas': writing to his sister just months before this act of 'betrayal', Clough darkly declares that soon 'Judas will be free to go and hang himself'.[14] Clough certainly thinks about hanging, he even (or almost) thinks about thinking *even as* one is hanging: 'I know I/ Yet shall one time feel the strong cord tighten ...'. This is Claude, and it is also Claude who, when frustrated in love and unable to think it all through, cries: 'HANG this thinking!'[15] Clough, we feel, could almost leave out the word 'this'. To quote *The Bothie*, Clough does not so much think *about* death as simply 'think death'; to put it another way, he seeks to think *through* death, in every sense of that phrase.[16]

Another nineteenth-century writer who does this is Dostoevsky who, just seven years after Clough's death, publishes *The Idiot* (1868); here the Idiot himself thinks through the experience of facing imminent execution:

> I ... imagine the most terrible part of the whole punishment is ... the certain knowledge that in an hour, – then in ten minutes, then in half a minute then now – this very instant – your soul must quit your body and you will no longer be a man. Who ... can suffer this without going mad?[17]

The answer may be 'no one', certainly not Dostoevsky who was himself sentenced to death before being reprieved at the very last moment, with the result that for the rest of his life he suffered epileptic fits. It may well be that the mind simply cannot bear the thought of death, that death, in the end, is literally unthinkable. In a very early poem on death, the young Clough declares, quite simply, that

I *cannot* think that all this light, this beauty shall depart.[18]

Clough always knew his attempt to 'think death' was doomed to failure; and when Clough cannot think he resorts, oddly enough, to walking; as Dipsychus says of God: 'It seems ... / We should not *think* of Him ... but *trudge* it.'[19] For Dipsychus, the problem of God is not something to be thought through but rather somehow walked through, and much the same goes for the sad and confusing fact of death. Using the word 'pace' where we expect the word 'think', Clough talks of how we must 'pace the sad confusion through', or 'walk and grimace it through'.[20] Clough is a poet who thinks on his feet; a keen walker, he speaks proudly of 'my philosophic foot'.[21] Clough has in mind that ancient Greek school of walking philosophers known as the Peripatetics (literally, 'those who walk'), so-called because they followed Aristotle who was famous for walking in the Lyceum even as he taught. The devout, undergraduate Clough is critical of what he calls 'Peripatetic Philosophy' but, by the time he is a don at Oriel, Clough is himself a Peripatetic, or at least so jokes Matthew Arnold when he sends Clough a letter addressed to 'Citizen Clough, *Oriel* Lyceum'.[22] Aristotle's Lyceum was the garden in Athens where he famously walked and taught, but the peripatetic Clough does his thinking-whilst-walking not in a garden but on a street: 'my philosophic foot shall greet', he writes, 'the dirt and refuse of thy street'.[23] Clough thus styles himself as a modern Peripatetic. To be more precise, he marks himself out as a post-Romantic, or urban, Peripatetic; whilst the eighteenth century ended with Wordsworth and Coleridge earnestly walking the Lakes and Alps, the nineteenth century witnessed the figure of the strolling urban intellectual, in particular the Parisian *flâneur* (literally, 'the stroller'). As Walter Benjamin writes, 'the *flâneur* provides [the city] ... with its [own] philosopher' or rather, *anti*-philosopher; to quote Charles Baudelaire, from 1863, 'the ... *flâneur* is an "I" ... which is always unstable and fugitive'.[24] Moving through the cafés, boulevards and arcades of the modern city, the *flâneur* is forever interpreting the city from different perspectives; his constantly distracted mind is constantly wandering. This is, quite splendidly, Claude in Rome: 'so through the city I wander and question'; it is also Clough himself in revolutionary Paris: 'I do little else than potter about under the Tuilleries Chestnuts and here and there about bridges and streets, *pour savourer la republique*.'[25] This is Clough very self-consciously playing the part of the *flâneur*, as he does again when declaring,

> I do prefer, I must confess,
> The somewhat slovenly undress
> Of slippered slip-slop sentimentals
> To Philosophic regimentals.[26]

Like the *flâneur*, Clough is a walking philosopher who avoids the regimentation of conventional philosophy. Clough's philosophic foot is slip-slop; that is to say, slip-*shod*, poorly shod. Clough's philosophic foot lacks precisely the sensible shoes made by Clough himself; in 1844 Clough compares his academic work to cobbling: 'I ... dress intellectual leather, cut it out to pattern ... and cobble it into boots and shoes.' [27] It may be that Clough always thought on his feet, but as he grows out of Oxford's academic boots so his thinking grows ever more slip-slop, slip-shod. Clough is quite literally slip-slod when, in July 1838, 'after 5 [continuous] months at Oxford', he takes a holiday in Penrith with his friend Thomas Burbidge; recalling these days of release, Clough sketches a scene that is at once both poignant and faintly absurd:

> One evening we went to the top of Place Fell, Burbidge without his hat, and with dancing shoes on, and I with slippers on.[28]

Once free of ponderous academic leather, Clough's feet become unpredictable, they begin to improvise. And this they do again, just a year later, when Clough, having taken the coach from Oxford to Braunston, suddenly decides to do the forty-mile return journey on foot; it was, he writes, 'a very rash experiment

... quite unpremeditated and accidental'.[29] Away from Oxford, long before he ever travels to Paris, Clough begins to walk like an improvisatorial *flâneur*; Clough's philosophic foot is quite capable of being unphilosophic or even anti-philosophic. And this is particularly true when it comes to death. When Dipsychus contemplates death's door, 'my philosophic foot' becomes 'my foolish foot':

> ...from my boyhood until now ...
> ...
> Somewhat has ever stepped in to arrest
> My ingress at the fatal-closing door,
> That many and many a time my foolish foot
> O'ertreading the dim sill, spite of itself
> And spite of me, instinctively fell back.[30]

Every time Dipsychus attempts to walk through death's open door, to think it through, his foot refuses, as if with a will of its own. Dipsychus's would-be philosophic foot is made foolish by death; or rather by the 'somewhat', or something that 'has ever stepped in to *arrest*' Dipsychus, to get in his way on the very threshold of death.

Dipsychus's Spirit is quite sure he can identify this mysterious, intervening other; recalling the bizarre Old Testament story of Balaam's ass (the ass that refuses to go any further when confronted by an angel that is invisible to his master), the Spirit tells Dipsychus: 'An angel met you in the way.' Naïve as ever, Dipsychus is all too ready to believe the tempter-Spirit: Dipsychus tells himself, ' 'Tis holy ground your foot has stepped upon.' And so it may be – the threshold of death was still, for many, intensely holy ground; but it was also intensely crowded ground. Back in the seventeenth century Andrew Marvell had declared, 'the grave is a fine and private place'; by the mid-nineteenth century it is neither.[31] With the massive increase in urban populations the churchyards in British cities were almost literally overflowing. To die at this time was to join a queue; to attempt ingress at the fatal-closing door was to find that others really have 'stepped in', have also got their foot in the door. To call up words from 'Mari Magno': 'So many feet there intervene.'[32]

WHERE

... where to seek the dead.

('Easter Day, Naples, 1849')[33]

In mid-century Britain the city is just one place where the dead intervene. There is also Ireland where, in the forties, famine kills a million in just four years; then there is the Crimea where, in the fifties, thirty-six years after Waterloo, Britain suddenly experiences a major conflict, losing 23,000 men in two years; then again, there is always infant mortality: every year around 100,000 children died before their first birthday; last, but not least, there is hell, with many still believing that, as Arnold reminds Clough, '1000s of mankind [were] to be eternally [damned]', condemned to everlasting torment.[34] Such over-whelming numbers go some way to explaining Claude's hyperbolic talk of those who 'die by the million or billion'; mid-Victorian death was, above all, a numerical phenomenon – a mass movement rather than private event.[35] It was not until 1867 that executions were held behind prison walls and, in a sense, all mid-Victorians died in public. The poor died either on the streets, in the workhouse, or in houses too small or crowded to allow privacy; whilst those who could afford privacy invariably chose to do without it, preferring to die with the whole family and, quite possibly, all the servants gathered around the death-bed. Few would have shared or even understood Martin Heidegger's existentialist account of death; writing in 1926 Heidegger makes the difficult but arresting claim that 'by its very essence, death is in every case mine', 'no one can take the other's dying away from him'.[36] For the mid-Victorian, death is rarely ever mine, partly because one dies in public and partly because the 'art of dying' required one to die in the style of others. This was a culture still saturated with the Christian idea of atonement, or sacrifice – the idea of one man dying for another, as famously secularized in Charles Dickens's *A Tale of Two Cities* (1859) where, at the height of the French Revolution, one man goes to the guillotine quite literally in the place of another man, pretending to be him. In Heidegger's words, he 'takes the other's dying away from him'. Clough, though, is no Dickens. Not a famed novelist but a diffident poet,

Clough is closer to aloneness, and thus closer to Heidegger's sense of death. In his Oxford diaries the young Clough writes painfully and intensely of 'an awful being-alone' and even of 'the "being alone" question'.[37] Dipsychus's Spirit asks, 'O did you think you were alone?' – the answer, at least for the young Clough, is most profoundly 'Yes'.[38] And what he fears above all is 'being alone with ... one's sins', in which case one is absolutely and finally alone, because separated from that ultimate companion, God.[39] Being alone to this degree can only mean *dying* alone. For Clough the devout undergraduate, this is an appalling fate – it is, effectively, hell; however, for Clough the sceptical don, to die alone represents a freedom to be very much desired: in 'The Questioning Spirit' Clough advances an almost existentialist manifesto, in which 'let me think my thought' and 'let me live my life' is followed, in the manuscript, by 'let me die my death'.[40] The published version of the poem does not include this final demand; Clough thus comes close to Rainer Maria Rilke's late-century plea for a 'death of one's own' but, in the end, withdraws as if such a death were too much to ask for in the 1840s.[41]

According to Heidegger, we have no choice in the matter – it is simply the case that death is a passage through which only one person can ever pass at a time. Clough is not so sure. Whenever Clough approaches 'the fatal-closing door' he finds that, at the very last moment, someone or 'somewhat has [also] ... stepped in'. This someone else turns, at one point, into Clough's fiancée Blanche Smith; writing to her in 1853 Clough expresses the peculiar fear that

> at the threshold of another world we should be stopped and parted and sent back separately.[42]

Clough sees or foresees a strange incapacity to cross the sill, or threshold, of death; again it seems that more than one person is attempting to go through the door. This coming together at death should not be a problem; death as a moment of union or reunion with loved ones is a perfectly conventional Victorian vision, and one that is reflected widely in Clough. He talks fondly of husband and wife 'together tottering to the grave'; dreams of 'the day/ When we shall all be mingled into heaven'; and announces that 'Each other, yet again shall meet./ Ah joy! when, with the closing street,/ Forgivingly at last ye greet!'[43]

Such unions and reunions would not be out of place at the end of a mid-century Victorian novel; what distinguishes Cloughean death is that its bringing together is not so much the work of affinity or harmony but rather a trick, or accident, of chance and serendipity. Love, argues the sceptical Claude, is no more and no less than chance meeting, or juxtaposition: 'JUXTAPOSITION', he announces, 'is great.'[44] Others tell him 'affinity [is] greater', but the street-wise Claude insists they are wrong, declaring, 'Lo, as I pace in the street … I can be and become anything that I meet with or look at.' The world of the *flâneur* is charged with intense yet wholly random connections or conjunctions, and for Clough this threatens to demystify death as well as love, two of the grandest themes of Victorian culture. Clough is daring enough (or urban enough) to find love in a chance encounter in a railway carriage: 'Beside me, – in the car, – she sat … fickle chance [had] … joined us.' He is also urban enough to see death in terms of two men who, having taken 'one street's two sides', finally 'meet … with the closing street': as Life's street narrows and closes so lives converge and overlap.[45]

This lesson is repeated in 'Last Words. Napoleon and Wellington' (1853), where Clough responds to the death of Wellington not by writing an ode to the Duke (as Tennyson does) but rather by making Wellington share the moment of death with his arch enemy, Napoleon – only half of the poem is concerned with Wellington's last words.[46] And even this is no easy task since, as Clough candidly remarks, 'the Duke didn't [actually] say anything…did he?'[47] Clough confesses that he has to imagine 'the words [Wellington] said, if haply words there were', and all Clough comes up with is something about doing your duty; the poem's almost comic point is that the duke has to have his last words scripted for him. The heroic Wellington is, in death, as unoriginal as the petit-bourgeois Claude who cries: 'Ah … let me sing the song of the shopman/ And my last word be like his.'[48] Let me die like a shopkeeper. We are a long way from 'let me die my [*own*] death'. This is more difficult than Rilke might think. In 1849 Dickens begins *David Copperfield* with the words, 'Whether I shall turn out to be the hero of my own life … these pages must show'; but Wellington, like the hapless Claude, is scarcely even the hero of his own death.[49] When it comes to life's final act, neither writes his own script.

71

One man who does (as Clough reminds us) is Samson, the biblical strong-man who, when captured, blinded and shorn of his strength-giving hair, takes revenge on his Philistine captors by pulling their temple down, killing both them and himself. It is Samson, hero of both his own death *and* those of the Philistines, that Dipsychus dreams of:

> And am not I …
> … a kidnapped child of Heaven,
> Whom these uncircumcised Philistines
> Have by foul play shorn, blinded, maimed and kept
> For what more glorious than to make them sport?
> Wait, then, wait, O my soul!, grow, grow, ye locks, –
> Then perish they, and if need is, I too.[50]

In 'Dipsychus Continued', after 'an interval of thirty years', this would-be Samson has neither perished nor caused anyone else to perish; it is as if his locks, his hair have not re-grown. Clough's hair certainly does not re-grow once he goes prematurely bald. Clough is no Samson, and knows it; when *Amours de Voyage* is published in the American journal *Atlantic Monthly*, its editor J. R. Lowell omits four verses that might have offended his more religious readers – Clough meekly accepts. As Lowell acknowledges,

> We should have pulled down heavier columns than ever Sampson [sic] did. It is pitiable.[51]

And so it is, but then much of Clough's life is pitiable. When Clough, to everyone's astonishment, did not get a first-class degree, he declared 'I have failed'; ever since, almost all commentators on Clough's life and work have echoed this judgement. It could even be said that he fails in death as well as life; though he often, as Biswas writes, 'think[s] of himself as a martyr', as one whose death will be, like Samson's, a heroic act of defiance, that is not quite how things work out.[52] In 1853 Clough grandly writes to Blanche about the difficulties in being known as a sceptic, 'I do … sometimes think that my course is one that must be walked alone.'[53] He is immediately put right; by return of post, Blanche writes, dismissively: 'Dear boy, don't talk anymore of being alone, in your heresy', 'would it do any good … to martyr yourself?'[54] Just fifteen months later they are married.

Clough's martyring days are clearly over, he is never again alone in his heresy, not even in death; when Clough dies he is buried in a Protestant cemetery near Florence that happens to contain the remains of another well-known heretic – the notorious American transcendentalist, Theodore Parker (1810–60), who had died just a year before. Though Clough made it clear that he had 'no particular love' for Parker, he it is that Clough happens to cite as an 'example' of the infamy attached to 'being alone in your heresy'.[55] It is a considerable coincidence that the American Parker and the English Clough, two lone heretics who never met in life, should end up in the same Italian cemetery. It is a coincidence that Dipsychus would scarcely have believed: 'Chance and resolve,' he declares,

> Like two loose comets wandering wide in space,
> Crossing each other's orbits time on time,
> Meet never.[56]

But Clough and Parker *do*. To quote an essay Clough writes at Rugby, they are like 'travellers that meet in the wide desert' and, in doing so, Clough and Parker confound any sense of the grave as a fine and private place befitting the heroic martyr.[57] Instead, death becomes a place of intersection, or rather *collision*, for if Clough and Parker are like Dipsychus's comets (and both are travelling at the times of their deaths) their meeting produces not stasis or stillness but yet more movement, or energy.

For all its stillness, Cloughean death does somehow involve a certain movement. When in 'Dipsychus Continued' the fallen woman melodramatically announces, 'I go – to die – this night!' her death is itself a form of going.[58] In 'Mari Magno' we read that 'travel's a miniature life'; by convention, it is also a miniature death, or a miniature *of* death.[59] As Hamlet declares, death is that 'undiscover'd country, from whose bourn/ No traveller returns'.[60] In the case of Clough, the dead or dying man quite literally travels – across Europe. And as he travels, so he writes 'Mari Magno', his unfinished poem of travellers' tales. Here we read, 'A wandering life his life had lately been'. With death so near, this reads like an epitaph.[61] Clough wandered right up to the last three days of his life, but the anxiety betrayed in 'Mari Magno' is that he will keep on wandering, that for heretics such as Clough life-after-death is also a wandering life.

73

At one point this anxiety quite overwhelms the poem; this is when, in 'The Clergyman's Second Tale', the middle-class Edward sees a prostitute and her client disappear into the city:

> He watched them in the gas-lit darkness go,
> And a voice said within him, Even so,
> So midst the gloomy mansions where they dwell
> The lost souls walk the flaming streets of hell.
> The lamps appeared to fling a baleful glare,
> A brazen heat was heavy in the air;
> And it was hell, and he some unblest wanderer there.[62]

When in Naples, Clough wanders 'sinful streets' with a pimp beside him; now in 'hell,' as if dead, Clough (as Edward) is still wandering sinful streets.[63] The wandering does not stop with death; Clough does not stop when he gets there, if only because there is no 'there'. For Clough, the afterlife is as much 'here' as 'there': 'And it was *hell*' – *here and now*, in the sinful streets. As Clough remarks, 'There is no Heaven but this! There is no hell [but this].'[64] The old Christian map of heaven and hell is folded back into the here and now; even Dipsychus claims to be 'a kidnapped child of Heaven'.[65] In Clough it is difficult to see where life ends and afterlife begins. It is a recurring Victorian riddle. As Christian belief is revised and rewritten so the mapping of death grows ever more ambiguous; for almost the first time, ordinary men and women die disoriented, without knowing where, if anywhere, they are going and what, if anything, will meet them. In 1859, Edward Fitzgerald announces, 'The stars are setting and the Caravan/ Starts for the Dawn of Nothing.'[66] As Stanley tells Clough, even the devout Thomas Arnold, on the eve of his death, writes in his diary, 'What is to follow this life?'[67] Might it be the Dawn of Nothing? Writing in 1848, Clough ask what happens 'if we die and come to nothing'.[68] Clough proceeds to answer his own question: 'If we give over dancing, it doesn't therefore follow that the dance ceases'; though we ourselves may cease to move, movement itself continues.[69] There may be little, or no sense of place in Clough's vision of death, but there is a profound and even enhanced sense of *space*, space in which to move.

This is no easy or glib sense of space; it may, at any moment, turn out to be nothing but empty space – so says Dipsychus, who insists that to believe in an afterlife is simply

> ... to mark off thus much air
> And call it heaven.[70]

The space of death is dangerous space; it may be space in which to move or dance, but it is also space in which to vanish – this air, we fear, is thin air. And in Clough, the dead do sometimes vanish; Clough, like many a Victorian agnostic, simply does not know where the dead have gone. Even on Easter Day, at the very spot where Christ was entombed, there is 'no word/ Of where to seek the dead'.[71] We do have clues: here and there is talk of 'footfalls in far rooms', 'strange conscious hauntings', 'tables [being] ... rapped', and 'other regions'.[72] Such intimations are very mid-century; this was a time when many were keenly seeking the dead at séances where they really did listen for footfalls in far rooms and wait expectantly for tables to be rapped. Clough, though, hardly ever touches on this huge craze; even his rapped tables actually come from a scene in *The Bothie* where the undergraduates are, in fact, simply expressing their appreciation for an after-dinner speech. In this case, the intimation of ghosts is itself ghostly, just a trick of language and association, what Clough himself calls a 'vocubular ghost', or ghost of a ghost.[73] Elsewhere, Clough talks of the 'weary ghosts' of academic study that haunt the undergraduate; the students are weary *of* these ghosts.[74] And Clough himself indicates a certain weariness and wariness of the whole otherworldly scene when he entitles one particular early poem 'Blank Misgivings of a Creature moving about in Worlds not realised'.[75]

These words come from Wordsworth's poem 'Intimations of Immortality' (1807), but Clough's poem is quite defiantly about intimations of *mortality*: 'Here am I yet, another twelvemonth spent.'[76] The unrealized world on Clough's mind is not so much the world beyond, but what he here calls the 'buried world below'. Written around 1840, in the early days of Clough's scepticism, the poem seems determined to revise Romantic transcendentalism, to rewrite Wordsworth for a whole new hard-headed generation.

The possibility of other, unrealized worlds does return to Clough later in life, but this time it is as a scientific dream; writing in 1854 to his American friend Charles Norton, Clough remarks:

> There's a book called the Plurality of Worlds, by Whewell I believe, which some people are praising. It professes to prove that there are, most probably, no inhabitants in any of the planets, stars or other bodies.[77]

Clough's interest in contemporary astronomy and the question of whether we inhabit a universe or pluriverse dates right back to his youth, when he looks to the stars and sees a 'million worlds'.[78] As a schoolboy, he also writes a set of sonnets called 'The Lunar Microscope'.[79] This was in 1835, the year in which the *New York Sun* newspaper created an international sensation by running a series of hoax articles claiming that Sir John Herschel had, from his observatory, discerned 'creatures like human beings';[80] whether or not Clough was aware of this, he is certainly keen to satirize what he calls 'modern ologistic fancifyings ... of suns and stars, by hypothetic men/ Of other frame than ours inhabited'.[81] These same fancifyings are again the target of Cloughean satire when Dipsychus's Spirit, taking on Christian evangelists as well as astronomical 'ologists', helpfully suggests

> ... send[ing] up missions, per balloon,
> To those poor heathens in the moon.[82]

There is, it seems, no place free of religionists; a heathen is not even safe on the moon. In fact, he might just be where spiritual dramas and questions are most likely. That at least is the gist of Gell's letter to Clough in 1844; at once both exasperated and awed by Clough's concern with the precise theological import of the Thirty-Nine Articles, Gell writes, 'you always do fly nearer the moon than I do ... in the upper regions of the metaphysical world'.[83] Gell speaks casually, but perhaps better than he knows, his vision of the theologian-as-astronaut being echoed nine years later when Clough himself considers an analogy between outer space and what he calls spiritual space:

> It may indeed be true, as the astronomers say ... that the heavenly bodies describe ellipses; and go on, from and to all the ages, performing that self-repeating, unattaining curve. But does it, therefore, of necessity follow that human souls do something analogous in the spiritual spaces?[84]

The answer, Clough implies, is 'No'; spiritual space is simply too unpredictable, too lawless to be compared to outer space, or at least to a fixed, Newtonian account of space. To us, reading at the beginning of the twenty-first century – after Einstein and relativity theory, after Hubble and the expanding universe – Clough's sense of spiritual space seems remarkably close to outer space; particularly when Clough declares that 'the spirit … is centrifugal', that, unlike 'the flesh [which is] centripetal' (moves towards its own centre), the spirit moves away from the centre, flying off in every possible direction.[85] A flood, as Clough elsewhere observes, 'hurries six ways at once'; my spirit, it seems, can hurry a thousand ways at once.[86] I am an expanding universe. For us today, this makes some kind of sense. We are used to thinking of ourselves in astronomical terms, as made up of the carbon remains of long-dead stars; we are also well used to cremation (only legalized in 1884) and to having our ashes thrown to the winds, our carbon returning to space. In 1906 J. M. Barrie has Peter Pan announce that 'to die will be an awfully big adventure'; a hundred years on, after a century of genocide, we have all but lost our sense of adventure.[87] If there is anything left of death-the-adventure then it is because of astronomy. Something of this is already apparent in Clough, with his vision of a centripetal spiritual space; as Clough loses his religion he too looks to an expanding universe in order to map death. There is not just despair but both astonishment and excitement in Clough's cry: 'no word/ Of where to seek the dead'.

DIG

> Here I see him and here …
>
> (*The Bothie*)[88]

There might just be one word or clue that Clough has as to where to seek the dead – that word is 'here'. If 'there is no Heaven but this' and 'no Hell [but this]', then the dead can be nowhere else but here and, indeed, the dead can be no-*one* else but ourselves. To quote Clough, 'I lie here in my little coffin.'[89] For Clough, death is not purely and simply part of the centrifugal, exploding work of my spirit; it is also part of the centripetal, imploding work of my flesh, or creatureliness:

> However powerful my centrifugal force ... I shall be certain to be recalled by the at least equally powerful gravitation of hunger and thirst, not to mention nakedness –.[90]

Clough is recalled to himself, to the centre, or dead centre, of himself by the almost banal fact of being flesh – its 'gravitation[al]' force literally earths, or grounds him. This is a fate strangely echoed just a few months later in *The Bothie*, where the unholy trinity of 'hunger, thirst and nakedness' becomes the equally unholy:

> Dig, and starve, and be thankful.[91]

This is the ironic advice given to coal miners by Philip Hewison, by which he means: *dig* underground; *starve* because paid so little; and *be thankful* if and when you find any coal. Hunger, thirst, and nakedness – dig, starve, and be thankful; Clough is rewriting such famous tripartite dreams of the spirit as St Paul's 'faith, hope and charity' or the French Revolution's 'liberty, fraternity and equality'. In Clough, these dreams cannot survive the centripetal, gravitational pull of flesh. Make no mistake, this is *earth*-bound gravitation: hunger, thirst and nakedness lead inexorably to the grave, whilst those that dig as well as starve are, in the end, digging graves – their own. And many were doing precisely that in 1840s Britain: both in Ireland where the starving poor dug in vain as their potato crops repeatedly failed, and in England where each year around 200 coal miners died in accidents underground.[92] By the 1840s Clough and his contemporaries certainly do have 'word/ Of where to seek the dead'; they are in the ground and are not going anywhere.

For Clough, death combined with soil makes for an almost unbearable stillness; or at least that is what Dipsychus sees when, of a sudden, as if looking at a garden, he declares:

> So still it is,
> The tree exhausts the soil; creepers kill it,
> Their insects them.[93]

A tree, soil, creepers, insects; what would usually be viewed as a scene of growth and animation is here viewed as a scene of near-total death, a killing field in which the insects kill the creepers, the creepers kill the tree, and the tree exhausts the soil. Though the death Dipsychus sees is everywhere it is so slow, so gradual, as to be invisible; so invisible, in fact, that it would normally be mistaken for life. In a letter written to J. N. Simpkinson, Clough talks of a friend 'dying ... fast', but here he seems to slow death down in an attempt to know what it is, or does; in just the scene before, the Spirit asks Dipsychus:

> Will you go on thus
> Until death end you? If indeed it does
> For what it *does*, none knows.[94]

For Clough, it is possible that death does not *do* anything; the lesson of Dipsychus's dying tree is that death is not so much something that is *done* to life as a process so gradual that it is an *extension, or aspect*, of life. As Dipsychus tells the Spirit, 'you'll [not] ... die outright/ You'll somehow halve ... it'. Clough too seeks to halve it when he decribes bereavement as 'half-death'.[95] For Clough, there are *degrees* of death; one can be less than dead, but one can also be more than dead: 'Abel is dead,' cries Adam, 'and Cain – ah, what is Cain? Is he not even *more* than Abel dead?'[96] Still more dead are those who starve: 'to famish', suspects Clough, '[is] worse than once to die'.[97] Claude too considers what it means to die more than once; when he imagines being suspended over an abyss, he declares, 'I die ten deaths.' Like Dipsychus's Spirit, Clough seems inclined to divide death up; in so doing, Clough seeks to dissect, or complicate, death. For Clough, it is quite possible to 'live dying'; he may well have in mind those who dig and starve, or perhaps Dipsychus's exhausting and exhausted tree.[98] He could equally be thinking of Christ; in Naples, on Easter Day, Clough declares of Christ, 'Though He be dead, He is not dead.'[99] Cloughean death here flies in the face of that most basic, Aristotelian law of logic: namely, that $A = not\ B$.

This law is very much at work when, writing in 1833, Carlyle announces:

> Memory and Oblivion ... Day and Night, and indeed all ... other Contradictions in this strange dualistic Life of ours, are necessary for each other's existence.[100]

Unstated, but understood as foundational, is the *Life–Death* dualism, the dualism which lurks behind every other dualism or opposition within Western philosophy, whether that be self and other, mind and body, consciousness and unconsciousness, and so on. When Clough dissects death, when he starts to complicate the life–death dualism, he thereby tampers with the foundations of Western thought. Life may be dualistic but, for Clough, death is not; particularly now that it is no longer neatly divisible into heaven and hell. In Clough, death only complicates our sense of category, or definition, and even, therefore, our sense that the world is made up of separate and distinct things, or entities. Clough's Adam asks, 'what is ... death?' Now, just three years later, Clough himself is asking, 'What is any thing?'; for Clough, the first question, the question of death, very much prompts the second question, the question of philosophy.[101] Carlyle talks of his 'Life-Philosophy', but in Clough we have something more like Death-Philosophy, a way of thinking that is shaped not so much by 'dualistic Life' as by shadowy, ambiguous death.[102]

All this is particularly remarkable at a time when philosophy is still dominated by the idea of Life, an idea, or ideal, that has much to do with Romanticism's stress on organicism, or the living whole; this can be seen not only in Carlyle but Hegel, with his stress on what he calls 'the life-movement of truth'.[103] For Hegel, if you want to think about truth you do best to think of the movingness of life; for Clough, you are best to think of the stillness of death. At times, this makes Clough seem quite conventional; Clough's cry, 'though I perish, Truth is so', concerns the fixed nature of truth as seen through the lens of death; this is truth made in the still image of death.[104] There is, though, more to this stillness: that which is still cannot move *of itself*, but (because still) it can *be* moved. When Clough thinks as one who is dead, there *is* stillness: 'I lie in my little coffin here – thinking'; however, there is also movement, in that the coffin is a steam-ship taking Clough to America – the 'dead' man is *being* moved, being transported.[105] This is a strange and recurrent theme in Clough, a poet whose fascination with traffic and transport (whether it be coaches, trains, ships or even air balloons) extends to the dead. Just like the living, only more so, the dead are parcelled up and moved around. As well as Clough in his steam-powered, transatlantic coffin, there is the dutiful citizen who, claims Clough, is so quiescent as to be, in effect, 'drawn in a Bath chair along to the grave'.[106] The almost absurd notion of a corpse-on-wheels recurs in *Amours de Voyage* when

Claude speculates as to whether a bridegroom would agree so easily to marry were it not 'for his funeral train which [he] ... sees in the distance'. By 'funeral train' Clough means the procession of mourners that attended any well-to-do Victorian funeral, but Clough also sees in the distance a funeral *steam-train* – by the mid-1850s coffins were often being transported by rail.[107] The most famous coffin to travel by train would be the very last coffin of the Victorian era, that of Queen Victoria herself.

Dead bodies have always been parcelled up and moved around, but, for Clough's railway generation, the transported corpse has an especial significance. Crucial here is the body of Arthur Hallam, whose death in 1833 prompted Tennyson's monumental elegy *In Memoriam* (1850); as the poem recalls, Hallam's corpse was carried from Italy to England by boat.[108] At the dead centre of the Victorian culture of death is a moved body. This body is first Hallam, then Victoria herself; but it is also Christ. On Easter Day 1849 Clough echoes one of the theories advanced to explain Christ's empty tomb: that the body was not resurrected but simply moved a second time – not just from the cross to the tomb but also from the tomb itself: 'What', asks Clough,

> If [He were] not where [the disciples] ... laid Him first ... [but]
>> Where other men
> *Translaid* Him after ... [109]

Even for Christ, death now means becoming a corpse that is moved, or moved on, like an object, or a vagrant – helpless and, above all, passive. And it is the sheer passivity of the dead and dying that most astonishes Cain when he is witness to the world's very first death; having just murdered Abel, Cain declares:

> ... I could wish that he had struggled more –
> That passiveness was disappointing.
> ...
> But he went down at once, without a word,
> Almost without a look.[110]

No less passive is mid-Victorian death. In the modern, bureau-cratized state that is 1840s England, the duty of the well-drilled subject is, says Clough, not only to 'be drawn in a Bath chair along to the grave' but, as he rolls along, to 'Try not, test not, feel not, see not'.[111] The transported and passive corpse (dying, like Abel, 'without a word [or] ... look') tells Clough all he wants to know about modernity – namely, that we are passive to the point of scarcely being alive enough to die:

> Moral blank, and moral void,
> Life at very birth destroyed,
> Atrophy, exinanition!
> ...
> Pure nonentity of duty.[112]

If modern life is destroyed at birth, when it comes to death there is no one 'there' to die, just a nonentity. No one dies. This philosophical-cum-satirical intuition of Clough's is put to the severest possible test by the subsequent death of his baby son:

> We have had and have lost a little boy – who was born suddenly and only lived a few hours.[113]

As Clough's friend Frederick Temple observes, the same day's newspaper notified readers of both 'the birth and the death'.[114] Six years later, Clough's wife gives birth to another child, a daughter; writing to Clough, she remarks of the still unnamed child, 'Baby seems to think it was always there'; baby may *seem* to think but, arguably, it does not – there is, in a sense, no 'it' to think.[115] When Clough's baby son, who remains unnamed, dies within hours of being born, we come very close to a strange and tragic sense that no one has just died.

Martin Heidegger was fond of the medieval proverb that 'as soon as man enters on life, he is at once old enough to die'.[116] This is a secret the Victorians knew only too well, the secret that death is an effect of birth, that we die of being born. Clough explores this secret through the fallen Eve. Looking down at the infant Cain, the first baby ever to be born, Eve bluntly states:

> Is born of us, and therefore is not pure.[117]

By this, Eve means: is born and therefore is *condemned to die*. Cain will one day be disappointed by the 'passiveness' of Abel's dying, but as one condemned to die he will himself die a passive death; it is not something that he will *do* but rather that will *happen* to him, in much the same way as birth. In Cain's case, death and birth should share the same grammar, both should be passive verbs, as is so nearly the case in: *is* born and *is* condemned. Since we are all Cains, all condemned to die by being born, death is not something we ever *do*. Again, no one dies. The twentieth-century poet Robert Graves famously wrote *Man Does, Woman Is*; however, in Clough 'Man *Is, Death* Does'.[118] Adam wants to know 'what death does'; Clough's answer is 'everything', or at least all the doing involved in dying. No wonder Clough should elsewhere speak of 'death's *work*'.[119]

It is true that Clough tries to do death's work, tries to make it an active verb: he casts himself as Judas-the-suicide; prays 'let *me* die my death'; and remembers those who 'dig and starve' – if anyone *does* death, does its hard work, it must be those who dig and starve. But Clough is not a miner; in his case, it is always: 'dig, and starve, and be thankful *it's someone else*'. Try as he might, the bourgeois Clough remains at a distance from the active doing of death; he does not hang, does not dig, does not starve. Even in the middle of a war-zone he does not fight, an irony of which Clough, like Claude, is keenly aware. Death in Clough is something that others do. In Vladimir Nabokov's novel *Pale Fire* (1962) a fictional poet called John Shade declares that it is 'only [ever] other men [that] die'.[120] This is a philosophical riddle or psychological trick to which Clough comes very close, and does so even when he is playing dead. Even then Clough manages to be the conscious one: 'I lie awake in my little coffin – thinking ... about somebody that is *fast asleep*'.[121] I may be in a coffin but it is not I who am dead.

Here Clough dies *thinking* of someone else. Clough's Christ takes this a step further; he dies thinking he *is* someone else, or at least with his followers thinking he is someone else. In the unfinished poem 'The Shadow', Clough dreams he encounters a Shadow, or 'Shade', who claims to be the man that his disciples mistook for God: 'I am that Jesus .../ Whom ye have preached, *but in what way I know not.*'[122] Jesus (to quote *The Bothie*) 'dies mistaken', mistaken for someone else. As the poem continues, it grows ambiguous and difficult to follow before finally seeming to contradict itself when the Shade is asked exactly who he is:

> And the Shade answered, that he did not know;
> He had no reading, and might be deceived,
> But still He was the Christ, as he believed.[123]

At first the Shade believes he dies mistaken for God, now he claims he *is* the Christ; it is as if he has grown to believe his own disciples, has died *himself* mistaken, himself 'deceived'.

According to Nabokov's Shade, it is only other men who die; the curious and difficult lesson of Clough's Shade is that we only ever die *as* other men. When Clough himself died, a death-mask was made; the lesson of the Shade is that every death is itself a mask.[124] The peculiar thing is that, in the case of the Shade, the mask seems to have stuck – he really seems to *be*, or have *become* someone else. 'Death [is] ... for what?', asks Cain.[125] Clough's cryptic answer is: to become someone else. This might just be what Clough means by 'another and impossible birth'.[126]

I had a cast taken of the head – not very good but I get fonder of it every day. The features came out so very beautifully after death ...

(Blanche Clough, November 1861)[127]

Notes

INTRODUCTION – A THIN POET

1. Michael Thorpe (ed.), *Clough: The Critical Heritage* (London: Routledge and Kegan Paul, 1972), 340.
2. The last book-length study of Clough was by Robindra Biswas in 1972 – see bibliography; see Katharine Chorley, *Arthur Hugh Clough* (Oxford: Clarendon Press, 1962), 324.
3. *The Poems and Prose Remains of Arthur Hugh Clough*, ed. Mrs Clough, 2 vols (London: Macmillan, 1869), i. 391.
4. Quoted in Chorley, *Arthur Hugh Clough*, 325.
5. Ibid., 323.
6. *The Oxford Diaries of Arthur Hugh Clough*, ed. Anthony Kenny (Oxford: Oxford University Press, 1990), 13.
7. *The Complete Poems and Plays of T. S. Eliot* (London: Faber, 1969), 75.
8. *The Bothie*, in *The Poems of Arthur Hugh Clough*, 2nd edition, ed. F. L. Mulhauser (Oxford: Oxford University Press, 1974), 82. Henceforth *Poems*.
9. Ibid., 79.
10. *Dipsychus*, in *Poems*, 259.
11. Quoted in Chorley, *Arthur Hugh Clough*, 324.
12. 'The Questioning Spirit', in *Poems,* 3 (my italics); *Poems*, 153, 7.
13. *Poems.*, 168.
14. *Amours de Voyage*, ibid., 114 (my italics).
15. Thorpe, *Clough*, 341.
16. *Dipsychus*, in *Poems*, 244.
17. 'Last Words', in *Poems*, 343.
18. *Amours de Voyage*, in *Poems*, 113; 'Come, Poet, come!', in *Poems*, 353.
19. *Dipsychus*, in *Poems*, 286.
20. 'Resignation – To Faustus', in *Poems*, 193.
21. *Amours de Voyage*, in *Poems*, 114.

CHAPTER 1. IN THE STREET: THE THOUGHT OF GOD

1. *Poems*, 22.
2. 'Come back again, my olden heart!', ibid., 11.
3. For further discussion of Clough and the Oxford Movement, see Robindra Biswas, *Arthur Hugh Clough: Towards a Reconsideration* (Oxford: Oxford University Press, 1972), 59–94.
4. *The Correspondence of Arthur Hugh Clough*, ed. F. L. Mulhauser, 2 vols (Oxford: Oxford University Press, 1957), i. 106. Henceforth *Correpondence*.
5. *Poems*, 124. According to Clough's wife he wrote an essay on the New Testament Saul in an examination for a Balliol Fellowship in 1842 – see 'Memoir of Arthur Hugh Clough', in *Poems and Prose Remains*, i. 22.
6. See Acts 9:1–20.
7. For more discussion of Clough and historical criticism of the Bible, see Biswas, *Arthur Hugh Clough*, 133–5.
8. *Oxford Diaries*, 44; *Dipsychus*, in *Poems*, 260.
9. *Poems*, 161.
10. Friedrich Nietzsche, *The Gay Science* (1882), trans. Walter Kaufmann (New York: Vintage 1974), 181; G. W. F. Hegel, *Philosophy of Religion* (1827), 3 vols, trans. E. B. Speirs (London: Routledge, 1968), iii. 91.
11. 'Blank Misgivings of a Creature Moving about in Worlds Not Realised', in *Poems*, 28.
12. Ibid., 29.
13. 'Look you, my simple friend', in *Poems*, 26; 'So he Journeyed and Came to Horeb', ibid., 162.
14. Søren Kierkegaard, *Sickness Unto Death* (1849), trans. Alastair Hannay (Harmondsworth: Penguin, 1989) 126.
15. *Correspondence*, i. 246 (my italics). For the context of this assertion see Christopher Herbert, *Victorian Relativity* (Chicago: University of Chicago Press, 2001), 124.
16. *Poems*, 94.
17. *Correspondence*, i. 114.
18 *Oxford Diaries*, 11, 12.
19. Ibid., 27; quoted in Biswas, *Arthur Hugh Clough*, 42.
20. *Oxford Diaries*, 65, 96.
21. *Correspondence*, i. 115.
22. *Poems*, 100 (my italics).
23. See Gillian Beer, *Open Fields: Science in Cultural Encounter* (Oxford University Press, 1996), 262, 276.
24. *Poems and Prose Remains*, 294.

25. Ibid., 302.
26. *Poems*, 17.
27. Ibid., 96.
28. Ibid., 202.
29. *Correspondence*, i. 168.
30. Ibid., i. 88.
31. Quoted in Biswas, *Arthur Hugh Clough*, 91.
32. *Correspondence*, i. 109, 97 (my italics).
33. See Biswas, *Arthur Hugh Clough*, 190.
34. *Correspondence*, i. 49, 67, 223n (my italics).
35. Quoted in Biswas, *Arthur Hugh Clough*, 123.
36. *Oxford Diaries*, 197.
37. *Poems*, 200, 204.
38. Ibid., 203.
39. See Luke 24:13–35.
40. *Poems*, 204.
41. *Correspondence*, i. 182.
42. *Poems* 373 (my italics).
43. 'Ye flags of Piccadilly', in *Poems*, 335.
44. 'Mari Magno', ibid., 387.
45. *Correspondence*, i. 84.
46. See Biswas, *Arthur Hugh Clough*, 24–5.
47. See Evelyn Baris Greenberger, *Arthur Hugh Clough: The Growth of a Poet's Mind* (Cambridge, MA: Harvard University Press, 1970), 67.
48. *Poems and Prose Remains*, 285.
49. *Correspondence*, i. 218; *Poems*, 261.
50. See Eileen Yeo, 'Christianity in Chartist Struggle 1838–1842', *Past and Present*, 91 (1981) 123–39; and Frank Paul Bowman, *Le Christ des barricades 1789–1848* (Paris: Les Éditions du Cerf, 1987), 11.
51. Matthew 26:35–6.
52. *Poems and Prose Remains*, 301.
53. Joss Marsh, *Word Crimes: Blasphemy, Culture, and Literature in Nineteenth Century England* (Chicago: University of Chicago Press, 1998), 78.
54. *Poems and Prose Remains*, 301.
55. *Poems*, 14.
56. *Correspondence*, i. 200.
57. Ibid., i. 207.
58. Ibid., i. 206, 209.
59. *Poems*, 8.
60. Adrian Desmond and James Moore, *Darwin* (Harmondsworth: Penguin, 1991), 301–2.
61. *The Poems of Matthew Arnold*, ed. Miriam Allott (London: Longman, 1979), 256.

62. Marsh, *Word Crimes*, 107.
63. *Poems*, 200.
64. *Correspondence*, i. 209 (my italics).
65. Ibid., i. 190.
66. *Poems*, 22.
67. Ibid., 270.
68. Ibid., 317 (my italics).
69. *Correspondence*, i. 227–8 (my italics).
70. *Poems*, 23.
71. *John Keats: The Complete Poems*, ed. John Barnard (Harmondsworth: Penguin 1973), 344.
72. Kierkegaard, *Sickness Unto Death*, 147.
73. *Poems*, 269.
74. Ibid., 247.
75. Ibid., 23 (my italics).
76. Ibid., 174 (my italics).
77. W. David Shaw, *The Lucid Veil: Poetic Truth in The Victorian Age* (London: Athlone Press, 1987), 129.
78. Ibid., 119, 136–47.
79. Ibid., 143.
80. *Poems*, 247 (my italics).
81. Ibid., 363.
82. See Plato, *The Republic*, trans. H. D. P. Lee (Harmondsworth: Penguin, 1955), 278–86.
83. *Poems*, 194.
84. Plato, *Republic*, 297–8.
85. Hegel, *Philosophy of Religion*, iii. 91.
86. See F. W. Palmer, 'The Bearing of Science in the Thought of Arthur Hugh Clough', *PMLA*, 59 (1944), 215.
87. Shaw, *Lucid Veil*, 261.
88. *Poems*, 19.
89. Ibid., 169.
90. Ibid., 103.
91. Shaw, *Lucid Veil*, 269.
92. *Poems*, 165, 169.
93. Kierkegaard, *Sickness Unto Death*, 59.
94. Ibid., 35.
95. Florence Nightingale, *Cassandra and other Selections from Suggestions for Thought*, ed. Mary Poovey (London: Pickering and Chatto, 1991), 42.
96. Ibid., 25, 40.
97. Ibid., 43.
98. *Poems and Prose Remains*, 295.

99. Quoted in A. N. Wilson, *God's Funeral* (London: John Murray, 1999), 29.
100. *Poems*, 313.
101. Thomas Carlyle, 'On History Again' (1833), in *The Works of Thomas Carlyle*, ed. H. D. Traill, 30 vols (London: Chapman and Hall, 1896–1901), vi. 169.
102. *Poems*, 351.
103. Nietzsche, *Gay Science*, 181 (my italics).
104. *The Swinburne Letters*, ed. Cecil Y. Lang, 6 vols (New Haven: Yale University Press, 1960), iv. 16.
105. 'The Old Man of Athens', in *Poems*, 476.
106. Nightingale, *Cassandra and other Selections*, 50.
107. *Poems*, 281.
108. Ibid., 116; *Poems and Prose Remains*, 363.
109. *Poems*, 5–6.
110. Matthew Arnold, Preface to *Essays in Criticism* (1865), in *The Complete Prose Works of Matthew Arnold*, 11 vols (Ann Arbor: University of Michigan Press, 1960–77), iii. 290 (my italics).
111. Quoted in Biswas, *Arthur Hugh Clough*, 119.
112. *Correspondence*, i. 246–7 (my italics).
113. Ibid., i. 124.
114. *Poems*, 169.
115. Jean-Paul Sartre, *Existentialism and Humanism* (1948), trans. Philip Mairet (London: Methuen, 1997), 34 (my italics).
116. *Poems*, 4.
117. Quoted in Valentine Cunningham, *Everywhere Spoken Against: Dissent in the Victorian Novel* (Oxford: Clarendon Press, 1975), 143.
118. *Poems*, 158.
119. *Poems and Prose Remains*, 295.
120. *Poems*, 284.
121. *Correspondence,* i. 143.
122. *Oxford Diaries*, 29.
123. Karl Marx, *Surveys from Exile*, ed. David Fernbach (Harmondsworth: Penguin, 1973), 299; *Poems*, 43.
124. *Poems and Prose Remains*, 390; *Poems*, 168, 69.
125. Ibid., 319.
126. *Poems and Prose Remains*, 391.
127. *Correspondence,* i. 221.
128. Ibid., i. 220.
129. Derek Attridge, Introduction to *Jacques Derrida, Acts of Literature* (London: Routledge, 1992), 18.
130. *Correspondence,* i.128n, 124.

131. The proverb 'each must bear his own cross' alludes to the Roman law that the person condemned to be crucified had to carry his cross to the place of execution.

132. See Robin Gilmour, *The Victorian Period* (London: Longman, 1993), 95.

133. 'Progress', in *Poems of Matthew Arnold*, 277; 'Before a Crucifix' (1871), in *The Poems of Algernon Charles Swinburne*, 6 vols (London: Chatto and Windus, 1911), ii. 85; 'Pilate's Wife's Dream' (1846), in *The Poems of Charlotte Brontë*, ed. Tom Winnifrith (Oxford: Blackwell, 1984), 4; Charles Dickens, *A Tale of Two Cities* (1859; Oxford: Oxford University Press, 1953), 260, and *Bleak House* (1853; New York: Norton, 1977), 243, 198.

134. Carlyle, *Works*, i. 178.

135. *Oxford Diaries*, 33.

136. *Poems and Prose Remains*, 425.

137. *Poems*, 200.

138. See Clough, *Selected Poems*, ed. Joe Phelan, (London: Longman, 1995), 258n.

139. *Poems*, 319.

140. Nightingale, *Cassandra and other Selections*, 230; Alfred Tennyson, *In Memoriam* (1850), ed. Robert H. Ross (New York: Norton, 1973), 71.

141. See Matthew 22:9; *Poems and Prose Remains*, 285.

142. 'Review of *The Soul*', in *Poems and Prose Remains*, 302 (my italics).

CHAPTER 2. A MAN KILLED: THE THOUGHT OF HISTORY

1. *Poems*, 72, 297.

2. Ibid., 565.

3. See Jean-Paul Sartre, *What is Literature?* (1948), trans. Bernard Frechtman (London: Methuen, 1950); E. H. Carr, *What is History?* (1961; London: Penguin,1964); Emmanuel Kant, 'An Answer to the Question: "What is Enlightenment?"' (1784), in *Kant: Political Writings*, trans. H. B. Nisbet, ed. Hans Reiss (Cambridge: Cambridge University Press, 1991), 54–60.

4. Karl Marx, 'Towards a Critique of Hegel's Philosophy of Right: Introduction' (1844), in *Karl Marx Selected Writings*, ed. David McLellan (Oxford: Oxford University Press, 1977), 89; Leo Tolstoy, *War and Peace* (1869), trans. Vicomte de Vogue (London: Heron, 1979), 446 (my italics).

5. Quoted in Jim Reilly, *Shadowtime* (London: Routledge, 1993), 18.

6. Thomas Carlyle, 'On History' (1830), in *Works*, ii. 84.

7. *Correspondence*, ii. 502, 462, 546.

8. 'Adam and Eve', in *Poems*, 180, 182.

9. Mark Pattison, *Memoirs* (London, 1883), 236.

10. James Joyce, *Ulysses* (1922; Harmondsworth: Penguin, 1986), 28.

11. *Poems and Prose Remains*, 347; 'Mari Magno', in *Poems*, 425.

12. *Correspondence*, ii. 373.

13. *Poems*, 72. Interesting in this connection is Isobel Armstrong's nice observation that 'Clough's emphasis is on the transformation of "palpable" experience rather than the direct representation of it. That is why, though it has the solidity and substantiveness of a novel, *The Bothie* is not simply a *Bildungsroman* in verse' (*Victorian Poetry* (London: Routledge, 1993), 185).

14. *Poems*, 109 (my italics).

15. Ibid., 108.

16. Friedrich Nietzsche, *Beyond Good and Evil* (1886), trans. W. Kaufmann (New York: Random House, 1966), 49.

17. Carlyle, 'On History Again', in *Works*, iii. 175.

18. *Poems*, 398, 369.

19. Ibid., 407 (my italics).

20. Ibid., 418 (my italics).

21. Marx and Engels, *The Holy Family or Critique of Critical Criticism* (1845), trans. R. Dixon and C. Dutt, Karl Marx and Frederick Engels, *Collected Works*, 47 vols (London: Lawrence and Wishart, 1975–95), iv. 142 / Karl Marx and Friedrich Engels, *Werke*, 39 vols (Berlin: Dietz Verlag, 1956–76), ii. 150.

22. *Poems*, 287.

23. Ibid., 185.

24. See ibid., 148–56.

25. *Correspondence*, ii. 499.

26. Ibid., ii. 498.

27. *Poems*, 408.

28. *Oxford Diaries*, 214; see Jean Lindsay, *A History of North Wales* (London: David and Charles, 1974), 105, 114.

29. *Oxford Diaries*, 83.

30. *Dipsychus*, in *Poems*, 238; 'Burnt Norton' (1935), in *The Complete Poems and Plays of T. S. Eliot* (London: Faber, 1969), 172.

31. G. W. F. Hegel, *The Philosophy of History* (1837), trans. J. Sibree (NY: Dover Publications, 1956), 103; Thomas Carlyle, 'Characteristics' (1831), in *Works*, iii. 32.

32. Djuna Barnes, *Nightwood* (1937; London: Faber, 1950), 77; quoted in Chorley, *Arthur Hugh Clough*, 235.

33. *Poems*, 89; *Correspondence*, i. 218.

34. *Poems of Matthew Arnold*, 256.

35. 'Mari Magno', in *Poems*, 427; *Oxford Diaries*, 245; *Correspondence*, ii. 515; 'Seven Sonnets', in *Poems*, 327; *The Bothie*, in *Poems*, 72.

36. Chorley, *Arthur Hugh Clough*, 235.

37. *Poems*, 160.
38. 'The Eighteenth Brumaire of Louis Napoleon' (1851), in *Karl Marx*, ed. McLellan, 25.
39. *Correspondence*, ii. 569.
40. John Goode, '1848 and the Strange Disease of Modern Love', in John Lucas (ed.), *Literature and Politics in the Nineteenth Century* (London: Methuen, 1971), 45.
41. *The Letters of Matthew Arnold to Arthur Hugh Clough*, ed. H. F. Lowry (Oxford: Clarendon, 1932), 79.
42. *Oxford Diaries*, 245.
43. *Amours de Voyage*, in *Poems*, 97, 103; *Correspondence*, i. 243.
44. *Correspondence*, i. 199, 198.
45. *Poems*, 157.
46. Ibid., 271.
47. As Biswas writes, 'Clough...became in time the slave of this imperious...woman...He tied up parcels, he looked up timetables, he acted as her courier' (Biswas, *Arthur Hugh Clough*, 460).
48. *Correspondence*, ii. 502.
49. *Poems*, 629.
50. Ibid., 94, 95.
51. *Correspondence*, i. 256.
52. *Poems*, 95.
53. Ibid., 106.
54. Victor Hugo, *Les Misérables* (1862), trans. Norman Denny (Harmondsworth: Penguin, 1982), 285.
55. *Poems*, 264.
56. See, for example, entry for Monday, 4 July 1842 – *Oxford Diaries*, 209.
57. *Correspondence*, i. 261.
58. *Poems*, 107, 116.
59. Ralph Waldo Emerson, 'History', (1841), in *Ralph Waldo Emerson*, ed. R. Poirier (Oxford: Oxford University Press, 1990), 115, 116, 121 (my italics).
60. C. Butler and C. Seiler (eds), *Hegel: The Letters* (Bloomington: Indiana University Press, 1984), 114.
61. *Poems*, 269.
62. *Correspondence*, ii. 348 (my italics).
63. William Shakespeare, *Hamlet* (1601?), ed. Harold Jenkins (London: Routledge, 1982), I. v. 196.
64. *Correspondence*, ii. 64, 499.
65. *Dipsychus*, in *Poems*, 255; Thomas Carlyle, *The French Revolution*, in *Works*, ii. 5.
66. *Amours de Voyage*, in *Poems*, 619 (my italics).
67. *Letters of Matthew Arnold to Arthur Hugh Clough*, 89.

68. Quoted in Chorley, *Arthur Hugh Clough*, 188.
69. *Letters of Matthew Arnold to Arthur Hugh Clough*, 63.
70. Thomas Carlyle, 'Signs of the Times' (1829), in *Works*, ii. 59; Edward Bulwer-Lytton, *England and the English* (1833), ed. Standish Meacham (Chicago: University of Chicago Press, 1970), 286.
71. Matthew Arnold, Preface to 1st edition of *Poems* (1853), repr. in *Selected Prose*, ed. P. J. Keating (Harmondsworth: Penguin, 1970), 41.
72. *Poems*, 269.
73. Quoted in Greenberger, 113.
74. Rebecca Solnit, *Motion Studies* (London: Bloomsbury, 2003), 7 (my italics).
75. *Oxford Diaries*, 253; *Poems*, 284–5.
76. *Poems*, 117.
77. Ibid., 270.
78. Carlyle, 'On History', in *Works*, ii. 83.
79. Matthew Arnold, 'Stanzas from the Grande Chartreuse', in *Poems of Matthew Arnold*, 305.
80. *Selected Prose Works of Arthur Hugh Clough*, ed. Buckner B. Trawick (Alabama: Alabama University Press, 1964), 308.
81. *Oxford Diaries*, 253.
82. Emerson, 'History', 114.
83. 'I said so, but it is not true', in *Poems*, 324.
84. *Correspondence*, i. 218.
85. *Poems*, 152.
86. Ibid., 718.
87. Ibid., 324.
88. *Oxford Diaries*, 254.
89. Walter Benjamin, 'Theses on the Philosophy of History' (1940), in *Illuminations*, trans. Harry Zohn (London: Fontana, 1973), 255.
90. *Poems*, 643.
91. Ibid., 789, 308.
92. Ibid., 63, 64.
93. 'As one who shoots an arrow overhead', ibid., 199.
94. *Poems*, 642, 125.
95. 'Commemoration Sonnets', ibid., 9; 'Blank Misgivings', ibid., 32.
96. *Correspondence*, i .284.
97. *Poems*, 181, 406, 398.
98. Ibid., 125.
99. Ibid., 394 (my italics).
100. Ibid., 284.
101. Quoted in Gillian Beer, *Open Fields: Science in Cultural Encounter* (Oxford University Press, 1996), 223.
102 *Poems*, 642.

103. Ibid, 364, 308.
104. Genesis 19:1, 10 (my italics).
105. *Poems*, 718.
106. Ibid., 351 (my italics).
107. Benjamin, 'Theses', in *Illuminations*, 249.
108. *Poems*, 343.
109. 'Ah, what is love', ibid., 565.
110. *Poems*, 710.
111. 'My beloved, is it nothing', ibid., 366 (my italics).
112. 1 Corinthians 13:12 (my italics).
113. 'What we, when face to face', in *Poems*, 341.
114. G. W. F. Hegel, *Phenomenology of Spirit* (1807), trans. A. V. Miller (Oxford: Oxford University Press, 1977), 111.
115. *Poems*, 343 (my italics).
116. *Correspondence*, i. 256; 'Salsette and Elephanta', in *Poems*, 141.
117. 'On Latmos', in *Poems*, 39.
118. *Poems*, 131.
119. Franz Kafka, *The Trial* (1925), trans. Willa and Edwin Muir (Harmondsworth: Penguin, 1953), 250.
120. *Poems*, 168.
121. *Correspondence*, i. 265.
122. *Poems and Prose Remains*, 354.
123. Hegel, *Philosophy of History*, 86.
124. *Correspondence*, i. 267.
125. Ibid., ii. 611, 322.
126. *The Letters of John Keats*, ed. H. E. Rollins, 2 vols (Cambridge, MA: Harvard University Press, 1974), i. 387.
127. 'Adam and Eve', in *Poems*, 169.
128. *Poems*, 105.
129. Quoted in Greenberger, *Arthur Hugh Clough*, 50, 49.
130. Ibid., 154–5, 157.
131. *Poems*, 119.
132. Ibid., 324.
133. Ibid., 116.
134. Ibid., 626.
135. See Leslie Williams, *Daniel O'Connell, The British Press and the Irish Famine* (Aldershot: Ashgate, 2003).
135. *Poems*, 170.
136. *Poems and Prose Remains*, 54.
137. *Correspondence*, ii. 504 (my italics); *Poems and Prose Remains*, 354.
138. *Poems*, 166.

CHAPTER 3. HANG THINKING: THE THOUGHT OF DEATH

1. *Poems*, 325.
2. 'Adam and Eve', ibid., 174, 183.
3. Ibid., 179 (my italics).
4. Isobel Armstrong, *Arthur Hugh Clough* (London: Longmans, Green and Co., 1962), 20.
5. *Poems*, 174, 717 (my italics).
6. *Correspondence*, ii. 326.
7. *Poems*, 648, 102 (my italics).
8. 'Seven Sonnets', ibid., 327.
9. Quoted in Michael Wheeler, *Heaven, Hell and the Victorians* (Cambridge: Cambridge University Press, 1994), 31.
10. *Correspondence*, i. 119.
11. See Biswas, *Arthur Hugh Clough*, 461, and Chorley, *Arthur Hugh Clough*, 321–6.
12. *Poems*, 102.
13. *Poems and Prose Remains*, 297.
14. *Correspondence*, 203.
15. *Poems*, 120.
16. Ibid., 610.
17. Fyodor Dostoevsky, *The Idiot* (1868), trans. Alan Meyers (Oxford: Oxford University Press, 1992), 23.
18. 'The Old Man of Athens', in *Poems*, 477 (my italics).
19. *Poems*, 268 (my italics).
20. 'What we, when face to face we see', ibid., 341 (my italics); 'Believe me, lady', ibid., 160.
21. 'Resignation – To Faustus', ibid., 193.
22. Quoted in Biswas, *Arthur Hugh Clough*, 76; *Correspondence*, i. 217 (my italics).
23. *Poems*, 193.
24. Walter Benjamin, *Charles Baudelaire, a Lyric Poet in the Era of High Capitalism* (1969), trans. Harry Zohn (London: Verso, 1973), 35; Charles Baudelaire, *The Painter of Modern Life and Other Essays* (1963), trans. Jonathan Mayne (London: Phaidon, 1964), 9–10.
25. *Poems*, 103; *Correspondence*, 206.
26. 'If help there is not but the Muse', in *Poems*, 159.
27. *Correspondence*, 140.
28. Ibid., 73.
29. *Correspondence*, 97.
30. *Poems*, 231.
31. Andrew Marvell, *The Complete Poems*, ed. Elizabeth Story Dunno (Harmondsworth: Penguin, 1972), 51.

32. *Poems*, 391.
33. 'Easter Day, Naples, 1849', ibid., 203.
34. *Letters of Matthew Arnold to Arthur Hugh Clough*, 55.
35. *Poems*, 626.
36. Martin Heidegger, *Being and Time* (1927), trans. John Macquarrie and Edward Robinson (Oxford: Blackwell, 1962), 284.
37. *Oxford Diaries*, 34, 5.
38. *Poems*, 273.
39. *Oxford Diaries*, 34.
40. *Poems*, 3, 546.
41. Quoted in George Steiner, *Heidegger* (London: Fontana, 1992), 104.
42. *Correspondence*, ii. 380.
43. 'The Silver Wedding', in *Poems*, 20; *'Sa Majesté Très Chrétienne'*, ibid., 671; *'Sic Itur'*, ibid., 9.
44. *Poems*, 118–19 .
45. 'Natura Naturans', ibid., 36; *'Sic Itur'*, ibid., 9.
46. See 'Ode on the Death of the Duke of Wellington', in *The Poems of Tennyson*, ed. C. Ricks, 3 vols (London: Longman, 1969), ii. 482.
47. *Poems*, 751.
48. Ibid., 631.
49. Charles Dickens, *David Copperfield* (1849–50; Harmondsworth: Penguin, 1966), 49.
50. *Poems*, 287–8.
51. *Correspondence*, ii. 537.
52. Biswas, *Arthur Hugh Clough*, 455.
53. *Correspondence*, ii. 365.
54. Biswas, *Arthur Hugh Clough*, 456.
55. *Correspondence*, i. 66.
56. *Poems*, 279.
57. 'Henry Sinclair, or 'tis Six Years Ago', in *Selected Prose Works*, ed. Trawick, 300.
58. *Poems*, 297.
59. Ibid., 391.
60. Shakespeare, *Hamlet*, ed. Jenkins, III. i. 80.
61. *Poems*, 397.
62. Ibid., 423.
63. Ibid., 203.
64. Ibid., 201.
65. Ibid., 287.
66. Edward Fitzgerald, 'Rubáiyát of Omar Khayyám', in *Victorian Verse*, ed. C. Ricks (Oxford: Oxford University Press, 1987), 350.
67. *Correspondence*, i. 119.
68. Ibid., i. 227.
69. Ibid., i. 227–8.

70. *Poems*, 240.
71. Ibid., 203.
72. 'Uranus', ibid., 193; 'Salsette and Elephanta', ibid., 143; *The Bothie*, ibid., 48; 'Mari Magno', ibid., 398.
73. *The Bothie*, ibid., 91.
74. *Poems*, 55.
75. Ibid., 28.
76. Ibid., 30.
77. *Correspondence*, ii. 473.
78. *Poems*, 471.
79. See Biswas, *Arthur Hugh Clough*, 55.
80. See Richard Adams Locke, *The Moon Hoax* (Boston: G. K. Hall and Co., 1975), *passim*.
81. 'Uranus', in *Poems*, 194.
82. *Poems*, 260.
83. *Correspondence*, i. 128n.
84. 'Review of Some Poems by Alexander Smith and Matthew Arnold', in *Poems and Prose Remains*, 378.
85. *Correspondence*, i. 201.
86. *The Bothie*, in *Poems*, 46.
87. J. M. Barrie, *Peter Pan* (1911; London: Hodder and Stoughton, 1951), 137.
88. *The Bothie*, in *Poems*, 65.
89. *Correspondence*, ii. 326.
90. Ibid., i. 201.
91. *Poems*, 73.
92. See Roy Church, *The History of the British Coal Industry*, 4 vols (Oxford: Clarendon Press, 1986), 586.
93. *Poems*, 287.
94. *Correspondence* i. 62; *Poems*, 284 (my italics).
95. *Poems*, 149.
96. 'Adam and Eve', ibid., 180 (my italics).
97. 'Was it this that I was sent for', ibid., 329.
98. *Dipsychus,* ibid., 713.
99. *Poems*, 204.
100. Carlyle, 'On History Again', in *Works*, iii. 173.
101. 'Recent English Poetry', in *Selected Prose* Works, ed. Trawick, 158.
102. Thomas Carlyle, *Sartor Resartus* (1833; London: Chapman Hall, 1910), 51.
103. G. W. F. Hegel, *The Phenomenology of Mind* (1807), trans. J. B. Baillie (New York: Harper Torchbooks, 1967), 105.
104. 'It fortifies my soul to know', in *Poems*, 304.
105. *Correspondence*, ii. 326.
106. 'Duty – that's to say complying', in *Poems*, 27.

107. *Poems*, 117; see James Stevens Curl, *The Victorian Celebration of Death* (London: David and Charles, 1972), 2, 141–2.
108. See *Poems of Tennyson*, ed. Ricks, 2, 327–8.
109. 'Easter Day', in *Poems*, 199 (my italics).
110. 'Adam and Eve', ibid., 179.
111. 'Duty – that's to say complying', ibid., 27.
112. Ibid., 28.
113. *Correspondence*, ii. 499.
114. Ibid., ii. 496 (my italics).
115. Ibid., ii. 596.
116. See Steiner, *Heidegger*, 104.
117. 'Adam and Eve', in *Poems*, 173.
118. Robert Graves, *Man Does, Woman Is* (London: Cassell, 1964).
119. 'Irritability Unnatural', in *Poems*, 161 (my italics).
120. Vladimir Nabokov, *Pale Fire* (Harmondsworth: Penguin, 1962), 35.
121. *Correspondence*, ii. 326 (my italics).
122. *Poems*, 371 (my italics).
123. Ibid., 372.
124. See Chorley, *Clough*, 326
125. 'Adam and Eve', in *Poems*, 180.
126. 'Easter Day, Naples, 1849', ibid., 202.
127. *Correspondence*, ii. 610.

Select Bibliography

WORKS BY ARTHUR HUGH CLOUGH

Editions, Poetry and Prose

The Poems and Prose Remains of Arthur Hugh Clough, ed. Mrs Clough, 2 vols (London: Macmillan, 1869). Includes several fascinating essays.

The Correspondence of Arthur Hugh Clough, ed. F. L. Mulhauser, 2 vols (Oxford: Oxford University Press, 1957). Invaluable, though not quite comprehensive.

Selected Prose Works of Arthur Hugh Clough, ed. Buckner B. Trawick (Alabama: University of Alabama Press, 1964). An excellent supplement to *Poems and Prose Remains*.

The Poems of Arthur Hugh Clough, 2nd edn, ed. F. L. Mulhauser (Oxford: Oxford University Press, 1974). Essential, though not flawless.

Amours de Voyage, ed. Patrick Scott (St Lucia: University of Queensland Press, 1974). Includes excellent annotation, both textual and explanatory.

The Bothie, ed. Patrick Scott (St Lucia: University of Queensland Press, 1976). Also includes excellent annotation.

The Oxford Diaries of Arthur Hugh Clough, ed. Anthony Kenny (Oxford: Oxford University Press, 1990). Fascinating, though only a selection.

The Poems of Arthur Hugh Clough, ed. Jim McCue (Harmondsworth: Penguin, 1991). A useful selection, but does not include the whole of *Dipsychus*.

Clough: Selected Poems, ed. J. H. Phelan (London: Longman, 1995). An excellent selection with very fine annotation.

BIBLIOGRAPHY

Gollin, Richard et al, *Arthur Hugh Clough: A Descriptive Catalogue: Poetry, Prose, Biography and Criticism* (New York Public Library, 1967).

BIOGRAPHY

Biswas, Robindra, *Arthur Hugh Clough: Towards a Reconsideration* (Oxford: Oxford University Press, 1972). Essential reading.
Chorley, Katharine, *Arthur Hugh Clough: The Uncommitted Mind* (Oxford: Oxford University Press, 1962). By no means made redundant by Biswas; particularly good on Clough's last months.

CRITICISM

Armstrong, Isobel, *Arthur Hugh Clough* (London: Longmans Green and Co., 1962). Brief but still very important in its insistence on Clough as an intellectual.
——*Victorian Poetry* (London: Routledge, 1993). Includes an excellent discussion of *The Bothie* in the context of radical politics.
August, Eugene R., '*Amours de Voyage* and Matthew Arnold in Love: An Enquiry', *The Victorian Newsletter*, 66 (1981), 15–20. A reading of *Amours* alongside Arnold's 'Marguerite' lyrics.
Bristow, Joseph, 'Love, let us be true to one another: Matthew Arnold, Arthur Hugh Clough and "our Aqueous Ages"', *Literature and History*, 4 (1995), 27–49. A persuasive reading of Clough and Arnold in terms of same-sex relations.
Dean, Paul, and Jacqueline Moore, '"To own the positive and present": Clough's Historical Dilemma', *Durham University Journal*, 45 (1983), 59–62. Considers the role of Eden in both *Dipsychus* and *Amours de Voyage*.
Dingley, Robert, 'Closely Observed Trains: The Railway Compartment as a Locus of Desire in Victorian Culture', *Cahiers Victoriens et Edouardiens*, 53 (2001), 111–39. Places 'Natura Naturans' in fascinating historical context.
Forsyth, R. A., 'Clough's "Adam and Eve": A Debating Tract for the Times', *Durham University Journal*, 53 (1992), 59–78. A very rare essay on a neglected poem.
——'Service on "the troublous tossing sea": Arthur Hugh Clough and the Journey of Life Topos', *Durham University Journal*, 56 (1995), 43–56. A good essay on an important Cloughean theme.

100

Gatrell, Simon, 'Histoires de Voyage: The Italian Poems of Arthur Hugh Clough', in Michael Cotsell, *Creditable Warriors* (London: Ashfield, 1990). Very good on Clough and the Victorian tourist.

Goode, John, *'Amours de Voyage*: The Aqueous Poem', in Isobel Armstrong (ed.), *The Major Victorian Poets* (London: Routledge, 1969). A very influential essay arguing that *Amours* is the major masterpiece of high Victorian poetry.

——'1848 and the Strange Disease of Modern Love', in John Lucas (ed.), *Literature and Politics in the Nineteenth Century* (London: Methuen, 1971). A fine essay on Clough and the tension between social structures and the individual.

Greenberger, E. B., *Arthur Hugh Clough: The Growth of a Poet's Mind* (Cambridge, MA: Harvard University Press, 1970). Includes excellent biographical detail.

Harris, Wendell V., *Arthur Hugh Clough* (New York: Twayne, 1970). A useful reading of Clough's spiritual biography but conforms to an all-too-linear narrative of Victorian 'loss of faith'.

Houghton, Walter, *The Poetry of Clough* (Cambridge, MA: Harvard University Press, 1963). A close reading, but tends to overlook historical contexts.

Kenny, Anthony, *God and Two Poets* (London: Sidgwick and Jackson, 1988). A study of Hopkins as well as Clough; important in its focus on Victorian Oxford.

Kierstead, Christopher, 'Where "Byron used to ride": Locating the Victorian Travel Poet in Clough's *Amours de Voyage* and *Dipsychus*', *Philological Quarterly*, 77 (1998), 377–95. A useful reading of Clough alongside Victorian travel writing.

Louis, M. K., 'Swinburne, Clough and the Speechless Christ: "Before a Crucifix" and "Easter Day"', *The Victorian Newsletter*, 72 (1987), 1–5. A nice comparative essay.

Maynard, John, *Victorian Discourses on Sexuality and Religion* (Cambridge: Cambridge University Press, 1993). Includes a startling chapter on Clough and the 'question of sex'.

Mermin, Dorothy, *The Audience in the Poem* (New Brunswick, NJ: Rutgers University Press, 1983). Considers *Amours de Voyage* in relation both to epistolary literature and the dramatic monologue.

Nadel, Ira Bruce, 'Kierkegaard and Clough', *Victorians Institute Journal*, 6 (1977), 4–37. A brief but fascinating essay.

Palmer, Francis W., 'The Bearing of Science on the Thought of Clough', *PMLA*, 59 (1944), 212–25. An interestingly timed essay on Clough and German thought.

Reynolds, Matthew, *The Realms of Verse 1830–1870* (Oxford: Oxford University Press, 2001) Includes a fine chapter on Clough as a resistant, even 'repulsive', poet.

101

Shaw, W. David, *The Lucid Veil: Poetic Truth in the Victorian Age* (London: Athlone Press, 1987). Places Clough in the context of Victorian philosophy.

——*Victorians and Mystery* (Ithaca: Cornell University Press, 1990). Includes a fine chapter on Clough, particularly good on Clough and consciousness.

Slinn, Warwick E., *The Discourse of the Self in Victorian Poetry* (London: Macmillan, 1991). Includes a good chapter on *Amours de Voyage*.

——*Victorian Poetry as Cultural Critique* (Charlottesville: University of Virginia Press, 2003). Includes a sophisticated chapter on *Dipsychus* as a challenge to traditional ideas of the self.

Thorpe, Michael (ed.), *Clough: The Critical Heritage* (New York: Barnes and Noble, 1972). An excellent selection of very early responses to Clough.

Timko, Michael, *Innocent Victorian: The Satiric Poetry of Arthur Hugh Clough* (Columbus: Ohio University Press, 1966). Makes valuable historical links.

Veyriras, Paul, *Arthur Hugh Clough* (Paris: Didier, 1964). Good on Clough's intellectual background, and includes some useful biographical material.

Index

Recent and Forthcoming Titles in the New Series of

WRITERS AND THEIR WORK

"...this series promises to outshine its own previously high reputation."
Times Higher Education Supplement

"...will build into a fine multi-volume critical encyclopaedia of English literature."
Library Review & Reference Review

"...Excellent, informative, readable, and recommended."
NATE News

"written by outstanding contemporary critics, whose expertise is flavoured by unashamed enthusiasm for their subjects and the series' diverse aspirations."
Times Educational Supplement

"A useful and timely addition to the ranks of the lit crit and reviews genre. Written in an accessible and authoritative style."
Library Association Record

WRITERS AND THEIR WORK

RECENT & FORTHCOMING TITLES

Title	Author
Chinua Achebe	*Nahem Yousaf*
Peter Ackroyd	*Susana Onega*
Kingsley Amis	*Richard Bradford*
Anglo-Saxon Verse	*Graham Holderness*
Antony and Cleopatra 2/e	*Ken Parker*
As You Like It	*Penny Gay*
W. H. Auden	*Stan Smith*
Jane Austen	*Robert Miles*
Alan Ayckbourn	*Michael Holt*
J. G. Ballard	*Michel Delville*
Pat Barker	*Sharon Monteith*
Djuna Barnes	*Deborah Parsons*
Julian Barnes	*Matthew Pateman*
Samuel Beckett	*Sinead Mooney*
Aphra Behn 2/e	*S. J. Wiseman*
John Betjeman	*Dennis Brown*
William Blake	*Steven Vine*
Edward Bond	*Michael Mangan*
Anne Brontë	*Betty Jay*
Emily Brontë	*Stevie Davies*
Robert Browning	*John Woolford*
A. S. Byatt	*Richard Todd*
Byron	*Drummond Bone*
Caroline Drama	*Julie Sanders*
Angela Carter 2/e	*Lorna Sage*
Bruce Chatwin	*Kerry Featherstone*
Geoffrey Chaucer	*Steve Ellis*
Children's Literature	*Kimberley Reynolds*
Children's Writers of the 19th Century	*Mary Sebag-Montefiore*
Caryl Churchill 2/e	*Elaine Aston*
John Clare	*John Lucas*
Arthur Hugh Clough	*John Schad*
S. T. Coleridge	*Stephen Bygrave*
Joseph Conrad	*Cedric Watts*
Coriolanus	*Anita Pacheco*
Stephen Crane	*Kevin Hayes*
Crime Fiction	*Martin Priestman*
Anita Desai	*Elaine Ho*
Shashi Deshpande	*Armrita Bhalla*
Charles Dickens	*Rod Mengham*
John Donne	*Stevie Davies*
Margaret Drabble	*Glenda Leeming*
John Dryden	*David Hopkins*
Carol Ann Duffy 2/e	*Deryn Rees Jones*
Douglas Dunn	*David Kennedy*
Early Modern Sonneteers	*Michael Spiller*
George Eliot	*Josephine McDonagh*
T. S. Eliot	*Colin MacCabe*
English Translators of Homer	*Simeon Underwood*
J. G. Farrell	*John McLeod*
Henry Fielding	*Jenny Uglow*

RECENT & FORTHCOMING TITLES

Title	Author
Veronica Forrest-Thomson – Language Poetry	Alison Mark
E. M. Forster	Nicholas Royle
John Fowles	William Stephenson
Brian Friel	Geraldine Higgins
Athol Fugard	Dennis Walder
Elizabeth Gaskell	Kate Flint
The *Gawain*-Poet	John Burrow
The Georgian Poets	Rennie Parker
William Golding 2/e	Kevin McCarron
Graham Greene	Peter Mudford
Neil M. Gunn	J. B. Pick
Ivor Gurney	John Lucas
Hamlet 2/e	Ann Thompson & Neil Taylor
Thomas Hardy 2/e	Peter Widdowson
Tony Harrison	Joe Kelleher
William Hazlitt	J. B. Priestley; R. L. Brett (intro. by Michael Foot)
Seamus Heaney 2/e	Andrew Murphy
George Herbert	T.S. Eliot (intro. by Peter Porter)
Geoffrey Hill	Andrew Roberts
Gerard Manley Hopkins	Daniel Brown
Henrik Ibsen 2/e	Sally Ledger
Kazuo Ishiguro 2/e	Cynthia Wong
Henry James – The Later Writing	Barbara Hardy
James Joyce 2/e	Steven Connor
Julius Caesar	Mary Hamer
Franz Kafka	Michael Wood
John Keats	Kelvin Everest
James Kelman	Gustav Klaus
Hanif Kureishi	Ruvani Ranasinha
Samuel Johnson	Liz Bellamy
William Langland: *Piers Plowman*	Claire Marshall
King Lear	Terence Hawkes
Philip Larkin 2/e	Laurence Lerner
D. H. Lawrence	Linda Ruth Williams
Doris Lessing	Elizabeth Maslen
C. S. Lewis	William Gray
Wyndham Lewis and Modernism	Andrzej Gasiorak
David Lodge	Bernard Bergonzi
Katherine Mansfield	Andrew Bennett
Christopher Marlowe	Thomas Healy
Andrew Marvell	Annabel Patterson
Ian McEwan 2/e	Kiernan Ryan
Measure for Measure	Kate Chedgzoy
The Merchant of Venice	Warren Chernaik
Middleton and His Collaborators	Hutchings & Bromham
A Midsummer Night's Dream	Helen Hackett
John Milton	Nigel Smith
Alice Munro	Ailsa Cox
Vladimir Nabokov	Neil Cornwell
V. S. Naipaul	Suman Gupta
Grace Nichols	Sarah Lawson-Welsh
Edna O'Brien	Amanda Greenwood

RECENT & FORTHCOMING TITLES

Title	Author
Flann O'Brien	*Joe Brooker*
Ben Okri	*Robert Fraser*
George Orwell	*Douglas Kerr*
Othello	*Emma Smith*
Walter Pater	*Laurel Brake*
Brian Patten	*Linda Cookson*
Caryl Phillips	*Helen Thomas*
Harold Pinter	*Mark Batty*
Sylvia Plath 2/e	*Elisabeth Bronfen*
Pope Amongst the Satirists	*Brean Hammond*
Revenge Tragedies of the Renaissance	*Janet Clare*
Jean Rhys 2/e	*Helen Carr*
Richard II	*Margaret Healy*
Richard III	*Edward Burns*
Dorothy Richardson	*Carol Watts*
John Wilmot, Earl of Rochester	*Germaine Greer*
Romeo and Juliet	*Sasha Roberts*
Christina Rossetti	*Kathryn Burlinson*
Salman Rushdie 2/e	*Damian Grant*
Paul Scott	*Jacqueline Banerjee*
The Sensation Novel	*Lyn Pykett*
P. B. Shelley	*Paul Hamilton*
Sir Walter Scott	*Harriet Harvey Wood*
Iain Sinclair	*Robert Sheppard*
Christopher Smart	*Neil Curry*
Wole Soyinka	*Mpalive Msiska*
Muriel Spark	*Brian Cheyette*
Edmund Spenser	*Colin Burrow*
Gertrude Stein	*Nicola Shaughnessy*
Laurence Sterne	*Manfred Pfister*
Bram Stoker	*Andrew Maunder*
Graham Swift	*Peter Widdowson*
Jonathan Swift	*Ian Higgins*
Swinburne	*Catherine Maxwell*
Alfred Tennyson	*Seamus Perry*
W. M. Thackeray	*Richard Salmon*
D. M. Thomas	*Bran Nicol*
Three Lyric Poets	*William Rowe*
J. R. R. Tolkien	*Charles Moseley*
Leo Tolstoy	*John Bayley*
Charles Tomlinson	*Tim Clark*
Anthony Trollope	*Andrew Sanders*
Victorian Quest Romance	*Robert Fraser*
Marina Warner	*Laurence Coupe*
Irvine Welsh	*Berthold Schoene*
Edith Wharton	*Janet Beer*
Oscar Wilde	*Alexandra Warrick*
Angus Wilson	*Peter Conradi*
Mary Wollstonecraft	*Jane Moore*
Women's Gothic 2/e	*E. J. Clery*
Women Poets of the 19th Century	*Emma Mason*
Women Romantic Poets	*Anne Janowitz*
Women Writers of the 17th Century	*Ramona Wray*
Virginia Woolf 2/e	*Laura Marcus*

RECENT & FORTHCOMING TITLES

TITLES IN PREPARATION

TITLES IN PREPARATION

Title   Author